T0215372

Python Packages

Chapman & Hall/CRC
The Python Series

About the Series

Python has been ranked as the most popular programming language, and it is widely used in education and industry. This book series will offer a wide range of books on Python for students and professionals. Titles in the series will help users learn the language at an introductory and advanced level, and explore its many applications in data science, AI, and machine learning. Series titles can also be supplemented with Jupyter notebooks.

Image Processing and Acquisition using Python, Second Edition
Ravishankar Chityala, Sridevi Pudipeddi

Python Packages
Tomas Beuzen and Tiffany Timbers

For more information about this series please visit: https://www.crcpress.com/Chapman--HallCRC/book-series/PYTH

Python Packages

Tomas Beuzen
Tiffany Timbers

CRC Press
Taylor & Francis Group
Boca Raton London New York

CRC Press is an imprint of the
Taylor & Francis Group, an **informa** business

A CHAPMAN & HALL BOOK

First edition published 2022
by CRC Press
6000 Broken Sound Parkway NW, Suite 300, Boca Raton, FL 33487-2742

and by CRC Press
4 Park Square, Milton Park, Abingdon, Oxon, OX14 4RN

CRC Press is an imprint of Taylor & Francis Group, LLC

© 2022 Tomas Beuzen and Tiffany Timbers

Reasonable efforts have been made to publish reliable data and information, but the author and publisher cannot assume responsibility for the validity of all materials or the consequences of their use. The authors and publishers have attempted to trace the copyright holders of all material reproduced in this publication and apologize to copyright holders if permission to publish in this form has not been obtained. If any copyright material has not been acknowledged please write and let us know so we may rectify in any future reprint.

Except as permitted under U.S. Copyright Law, no part of this book may be reprinted, reproduced, transmitted, or utilized in any form by any electronic, mechanical, or other means, now known or hereafter invented, including photocopying, microfilming, and recording, or in any information storage or retrieval system, without written permission from the publishers.

For permission to photocopy or use material electronically from this work, access www. copyright.com or contact the Copyright Clearance Center, Inc. (CCC), 222 Rosewood Drive, Danvers, MA 01923, 978-750-8400. For works that are not available on CCC please contact mpkbookspermissions@tandf.co.uk

Trademark notice: Product or corporate names may be trademarks or registered trademarks and are used only for identification and explanation without intent to infringe.

ISBN: 978-1-032-03825-4 (hbk)
ISBN: 978-1-032-02944-3 (pbk)
ISBN: 978-1-003-18925-1 (ebk)

DOI: 10.1201/9781003189251

Publisher's note: This book has been prepared from camera-ready copy provided by the authors.

To you, the Reader.

Never stop learning. You are capable of anything.

Contents

List of Figures

List of Tables

Preface

Python packages are the fundamental units of shareable code in Python. Packages make it easy to organize, reuse, and maintain your code, as well as share it between projects, with your colleagues, and with the wider Python community. *Python Packages* is an open-source book that describes modern and efficient workflows for creating Python packages. The focus of this book is overwhelmingly practical; we will demonstrate methods and tools you can use to develop and maintain packages quickly, reproducibly, and with as much automation as possible — so you can focus on writing and sharing code!

Why read this book?

Despite their importance, packages can be difficult to understand and cumbersome to create for beginners and seasoned developers alike. This book aims to describe the packaging process at an accessible and practical level for data scientists, developers, and programmers. Along the way, we'll develop a real Python package and will explore all the key elements of Python packaging, including: creating a package file and directory structure, when and why to write tests and documentation, and how to maintain and update your package with the help of automated continuous integration and continuous deployment (CI/CD) pipelines.

By reading this book, you will:

- Understand what Python packages are, and when and why you should use them.
- Be able to build your own Python package from scratch.
- Learn how to document your Python code and packages.
- Write software tests for your code and automate them.
- Learn how to release your package on the Python Package Index (PyPI) and discover best practices for updating and versioning your code.
- Implement CI/CD workflows to build, test, and deploy your package automatically.
- Get tips on Python coding style, best-practice packaging workflows, and other useful development tools.

Structure of the book

Chapter 1: Introduction first gives a brief introduction to packages in Python and why you should know how to make them.

Chapter 2: System setup describes how to set up your development environment to develop packages and follow the examples in this book.

In **Chapter 3: How to package a Python**, we develop an example package from beginning-to-end as a practical demonstration of the key steps involved in the packaging process. This chapter forms the foundation of the book and will act as a reference sheet for readers creating packages in the future.

The remaining chapters then go into more detail about each step in this process, organized roughly in their order in the workflow:

- **Chapter 4: Package structure and distribution**
- **Chapter 5: Testing**
- **Chapter 6: Documentation**
- **Chapter 7: Releasing and versioning**
- **Chapter 8: Continuous integration and deployment**

Assumptions

While this book aims to introduce Python packaging at a beginner level, we assume readers have basic familiarity with the concepts listed in Table 0.1:

TABLE 0.1: Concepts this book assumes readers have basic familiarity with.

Item	Learning resources
How to import Python packages with the `import` statement	Python documentation
How to write conditionals (`if`/`elif`/`else`) and loops (`for`)	Python documentation
How to use and write Python functions	*Plotting and Programming in Python: Writing Functions* (The Carpentries, 2021)
(Optional) Basic familiarity with version control and Git and GitHub (or similar tools)	*Happy Git and GitHub for the useR* (Bryan et al., 2021) or *Research Software Engineering with Python* (Irving et al., 2021)

Conventions

Throughout this book we use foo() to refer to functions, bar for inline commands/variables/function parameters/package names, and __init__.py and src/ to refer to files and directories respectively.

Commands entered at the command line appear as below, with $ indicating the command prompt:

```
$ mkdir my-first-package
$ cd my-first-package
$ python
```

Code entered in a Python interpreter looks like this:

```
>>> import math
>>> round(math.pi, 3)
```

```
3.142
```

Code blocks appear as below:

```python
def is_even(n):
    """Check if n is even."""
    if n % 2 == 0:
        return True
    else:
        return False
```

If you are reading an electronic version of the book, e.g., https://py-pkgs.org, all code is rendered so that you can easily copy and paste directly from your browser to your Python interpreter or editor.

Persistence

The Python software ecosystem is constantly evolving. While we aim to make the packaging workflows and concepts discussed in this book tool-agnostic, the tools we do use in the book may have been updated by the time you read it. If the maintainers of these tools are doing the right thing by documenting, versioning, and properly deprecating their code (we'll explore these concepts ourselves in **Chapter 7: Releasing and versioning**), then it should be straightforward to adapt any outdated code in the book.

Colophon

This book was written in JupyterLab[1] and compiled using Jupyter Book[2]. The source is hosted on GitHub[3] and is deployed online at `https://py-pkgs.org` with Netlify[4].

Acknowledgments

We'd like to thank everyone that has contributed to the development of *Python Packages*. This is an open source book that began as supplementary material for the University of British Columbia's Master of Data Science program and was subsequently developed openly on GitHub where it has been read, revised, and supported by many students, educators, practitioners and hobbyists. Without you all, this book wouldn't be nearly as good as it is, and we are deeply grateful. A special thanks to those who have contributed to or provided feedback on the text via GitHub (in alphabetical order of GitHub username): `benjy765`, `Carreau`, `chendaniely`, `dcslagel`, `eliasdabbas`, `fegue`, `firasm`, `Midnighter`, `mtkerbeR`, `NickleDave`, `SamEdwardes`, `tarensanders`.

The scope and intent of this book was inspired by the fantastic *R Packages*[5] (Wickham and Bryan, 2015) book written by Hadley Wickham and Jenny Bryan, a book that has been a significant resource for the R community over the years. We hope that *Python Packages* will eventually play a similar role in the Python community.

---

[1]`https://jupyterlab.readthedocs.io/en/stable/index.html`
[2]`https://jupyterbook.org/intro.html`
[3]`https://github.com/UBC-MDS/py-pkgs`
[4]`https://www.netlify.com/`
[5]`https://r-pkgs.org`

About the authors

Tomas Beuzen is a data scientist and educator based in Sydney, Australia. He has a background in coastal engineering and climate science and was a teaching fellow in the Master of Data Science program (Vancouver Option) at the University of British Columbia. Tomas currently works as a data scientist in the renewable energy sector and enjoys spending his free time developing open-source, educational data science material, and using data science to solve problems in the natural and engineered world.

Tiffany Timbers is an Assistant Professor of Teaching in the Department of Statistics and a Co-Director for the Master of Data Science program (Vancouver Option) at the University of British Columbia. In these roles she teaches and develops curriculum around the responsible application of data science to solve real-world problems. One of her favorite courses she teaches is a graduate course on collaborative software development, which focuses on teaching how to create R and Python packages using modern tools and workflows.

1

Introduction

Python packages are a core element of the Python programming language and are how you write reusable and shareable code in Python. This book assumes that readers are familiar with how to install a package using a package installer like `pip` or `conda`, and how to import and use it with the help of the `import` statement in Python.

For example, the command below uses `pip` to install `numpy` (Harris et al., 2020), the core scientific computing package for Python:

```
$ pip install numpy
```

Once the package is installed, it can be used in a Python interpreter. For example, to round pi to three decimal places:

```
$ python
```

```
>>> import numpy as np
>>> np.round(np.pi, decimals=3)
```

```
3.142
```

At a minimum, a package bundles together code (such as functions, classes, variables, or scripts) so that it can be easily reused across different projects. However, packages are typically also supported by extra content such as documentation and tests, which become exponentially more important if you wish to share your package with others.

As of January 2022, there are over 350,000 packages available on the Python Package Index (PyPI)[1], the official online software repository for Python. Packages are a key reason why Python is such a powerful and widely used programming language. The chances are that someone has already solved a problem that you're working on, and you can benefit from their work by downloading and installing their package. Put simply, packages are how you make

---

[1]https://pypi.org

DOI: 10.1201/9781003189251-1

it as easy as possible to use, maintain, share, and collaborate on Python code with others, whether they be your friends, work colleagues, the world, or your future self!

Even if you never intend to share your code with others, making packages will ultimately save you time. Packages make it significantly easier for you to reuse and maintain your code within a project and across different projects. After programming for some time, most people will eventually reach a point where they want to reuse code from one project in another. For beginners, in particular, this is something often accomplished by copying-and-pasting existing code into the new project. Despite being inefficient, this practice also makes it difficult to improve and maintain your code across projects. Creating a simple Python package will solve these problems.

Regardless of your motivation, the goal of this book is to show you how to easily develop Python packages. The focus is overwhelmingly practical — we will leverage modern methods and tools to develop and maintain packages efficiently, reproducibly, and with as much automation as possible, so you can focus on writing and sharing code. Along the way, we'll also enlighten some interesting and relevant lower-level details of Python packaging and the Python programming language.

1.1   Why you should create packages

There are many reasons why you should develop Python packages!

- To effectively share your code with others.
- They save you time. Even if you don't intend to share your package with others, they help you easily reuse and maintain your code across multiple projects.
- They force you to organize and document your code, such that it can be easily understood and used at a later time.
- They isolate dependencies for your code and improve its reproducibility.
- They are a good way to practice writing good code.
- Packages can be used to effectively bundle up reproducible data analysis and programming projects.
- Finally, developing and distributing packages supports the Python ecosystem and other Python users who can benefit from your work.

2

System setup

If you intend to follow along with the code presented in this book, we recommend you follow these setup instructions so that you will run into fewer technical issues.

2.1 The command-line interface

A command-line interface (CLI) is a text-based interface used to interact with your computer. We'll be using a CLI for various tasks throughout this book. We'll assume Mac and Linux users are using the "Terminal" and Windows users are using the "Anaconda Prompt" (which we'll install in the next section) as a CLI.

2.2 Installing software

Section 2.2.1 and **Section 2.2.2** describe how to install the software you'll need to develop a Python package and follow along with the text and examples in this book. However, we also support an alternative setup with Docker that has everything you need already installed to get started. The Docker approach is recommended for anyone that runs into issues installing or using any of the software below on their specific operating system, or anyone who would simply prefer to use Docker — if that's you, skip to **Section 2.3** for now, and we'll describe the Docker setup later in **Section 2.6**.

2.2.1 Installing Python

We recommend installing the latest version of Python via the Miniconda distribution by following the instructions in the Miniconda documentation[1]. Miniconda is a lightweight version of the popular Anaconda distribution. If you

---

[1]https://docs.conda.io/en/latest/miniconda.html

have previously installed the Anaconda or Miniconda distribution feel free to skip to **Section 2.2.2**.

If you are unfamiliar with Miniconda and Anaconda, they are distributions of Python that also include the conda package and environment manager, and a number of other useful packages. The difference between Anaconda and Miniconda is that Anaconda installs over 250 additional packages (many of which you might never use), while Miniconda is a much smaller distribution that comes bundled with just a few key packages; you can then install additional packages as you need them using the command conda install.

conda is a piece of software that supports the process of installing and updating software (like Python packages). It is also an environment manager, which is the key function we'll be using it for in this book. An environment manager helps you create "virtual environments" on your machine, where you can safely install different packages and their dependencies in an isolated location. Installing all the packages you need in the same place (i.e., the system default location) can be problematic because different packages often depend on different versions of the same dependencies; as you install more packages, you'll inevitably get conflicts between dependencies, and your code will start to break. Virtual environments help you compartmentalize and isolate the packages you are using for different projects to avoid this issue. You can read more about virtual environments in the conda documentation[2]. While alternative package and environment managers exist, we choose to use conda in this book because of its popularity, ease-of-use, and ability to handle any software stack (not just Python).

2.2.2   Install packaging software

Once you've installed the Miniconda distribution, ensure that Python and conda are up to date by running the following command at the command line:

```
$ conda update --all
```

Now we'll install the two main pieces of software we'll be using to help us create Python packages in this book:

1. poetry[3]: software that will help us build our own Python packages. poetry is under active development, thus we recommend referring to the official poetry documentation[4] for detailed installation instructions and support.

---

[2]https://conda.io/projects/conda/en/latest/user-guide/concepts/environments.html
[3]https://python-poetry.org/
[4]https://python-poetry.org/docs/

2. cookiecutter[5]: software that will help us create packages from pre-made templates. It can be installed with conda as follows:

```
$ conda install -c conda-forge cookiecutter
```

2.3 Register for a PyPI account

The Python Package Index (PyPI) is the official online software repository for Python. A software repository is a storage location for downloadable software, like Python packages. In this book we'll be publishing a package to PyPI. Before publishing packages to PyPI, it is typical to "test drive" their publication on TestPyPI, which is a test version of PyPI. To follow along with this book, you should register for a TestPyPI account on the TestPyPI website[6] and a PyPI account on the PyPI website[7].

2.4 Set up Git and GitHub

If you're not using a version control system, we highly recommend you get into the habit! A version control system tracks changes to the file(s) of your project in a clear and organized way (no more "document_1.doc", "document_1_new.doc", "document_final.doc", etc.). As a result, a version control system contains a full history of all the revisions made to your project, which you can view and retrieve at any time. You don't *need* to use or be familiar with version control to read this book, but if you're serious about creating Python packages, version control will become an invaluable part of your workflow, so now is a good time to learn!

There are many version control systems available, but the most common is Git and we'll be using it throughout this book. You can download Git by following the instructions in the Git documentation[8]. Git helps track changes to a project on a local computer, but what if we want to collaborate with others? Or, what happens if your computer crashes and you lose all your work? That's where GitHub comes in. GitHub is one of many online services for hosting Git-managed projects. GitHub helps you create an online copy of

---

[5]https://github.com/cookiecutter/cookiecutter

[6]https://test.pypi.org/account/register/

[7]https://pypi.org/account/register/

[8]https://git-scm.com/book/en/v2/Getting-Started-Installing-Git

your local Git repository, which acts as a backup of your local work and allows others to easily and transparently collaborate on your project. You can sign up for a free GitHub account on the GitHub website[9]. Once signed up, you should also set up SSH authentication to help push and pull files from GitHub by following the steps in the official GitHub documentation[10].

We assume that those who choose to follow the optional version control sections of this book have basic familiarity with Git and GitHub (or equivalent). Two excellent learning resources are *Happy Git and GitHub for the useR*[11] (Bryan et al., 2021) and *Research Software Engineering with Python*[12] (Irving et al., 2021).

2.5   Python integrated development environments

A Python integrated development environment (IDE) will make the process of creating Python packages significantly easier. An IDE is a piece of software that provides advanced functionality for code development, such as directory and file creation and navigation, autocomplete, debugging, and syntax highlighting, to name a few. An IDE will save you time and help you write better code. Commonly used free Python IDEs include Visual Studio Code[13], Atom[14], Sublime Text[15], Spyder[16], and PyCharm Community Edition[17]. For those more familiar with the Jupyter ecosystem, JupyterLab[18] is a suitable browser-based IDE. Finally, for the R community, the RStudio IDE[19] also supports Python.

You'll be able to follow along with the examples presented in this book regardless of what IDE you choose to develop your Python code in. If you don't know which IDE to use, we recommend starting with Visual Studio Code. Below we briefly describe how to set up Visual Studio Code, JupyterLab, and RStudio as Python IDEs (these are the IDEs we personally use in our day-to-day work). If you'd like to use Docker to help develop Python packages and follow along with this book, we'll describe how to do so with Visual Studio Code or JupyterLab in **Section 2.6**.

---

[9]https://www.github.com
[10]https://docs.github.com/en/authentication/connecting-to-github-with-ssh
[11]https://happygitwithr.com
[12]https://merely-useful.tech/py-rse/git-cmdline.html
[13]https://code.visualstudio.com/
[14]https://atom.io/
[15]https://www.sublimetext.com/
[16]https://www.spyder-ide.org/
[17]https://www.jetbrains.com/pycharm/
[18]https://jupyter.org/
[19]https://rstudio.com/products/rstudio/download/

2.5.1 Visual Studio Code

You can download Visual Studio Code (VS Code) from the Visual Studio Code website[20]. Once you've installed VS Code, you should install the "Python" extension from the VS Code Marketplace. To do this, follow the steps listed below and illustrated in Fig. 2.1:

1. Open the Marketplace by clicking the *Extensions* tab on the VS Code activity bar.
2. Search for "Python" in the search bar.
3. Select the extension named "Python" and then click *Install*.

FIGURE 2.1: Installing the Python extension in Visual Studio Code.

Once this is done, you have everything you need to start creating packages! For example, you can create files and directories from the *File Explorer* tab on the VS Code activity bar, and you can open up an integrated CLI by selecting *Terminal* from the *View* menu. Fig. 2.2 shows an example of executing a Python *.py* file from the command line in VS Code.

We recommend you take a look at the VS Code Getting Started Guide[21] to learn more about using VS Code. While you don't need to install any additional extensions to start creating packages in VS Code, there are many

---

[20]https://code.visualstudio.com/
[21]https://code.visualstudio.com/docs

FIGURE 2.2: Executing a simple Python file called hello-world.py from the integrated terminal in Visual Studio Code.

extensions available that can support and streamline your programming workflows in VS Code. Below are a few we recommend installing to support the workflows we use in this book (you can search for and install these from the "Marketplace" as we did earlier):

- Python Docstring Generator[22]: an extension to quickly generate documentation strings (docstrings) for Python functions.
- Markdown All in One[23]: an extension that provides keyboard shortcuts, automatic table of contents, and preview functionality for Markdown files. Markdown[24] is a plain-text markup language that we'll use and learn about in this book.

2.5.2   JupyterLab

For those comfortable in the Jupyter ecosystem feel free to stay there to create your Python packages! JupyterLab is a browser-based IDE that supports all of the core functionality we need to create packages. As per the JupyterLab installation instructions[25], you can install JupyterLab with:

---

[22]https://marketplace.visualstudio.com/items?itemName=njpwerner.autodocstring
[23]https://marketplace.visualstudio.com/items?itemName=yzhang.markdown-all-in-one
[24]https://www.markdownguide.org
[25]https://jupyterlab.readthedocs.io/en/stable/getting_started/installation.html

```
$ conda install -c conda-forge jupyterlab
```

Once installed, you can launch JupyterLab from your current directory by typing the following command in your terminal:

```
$ jupyter lab
```

In JupyterLab, you can create files and directories from the *File Browser* and can open up an integrated terminal from the *File* menu. Fig. 2.3 shows an example of executing a Python *.py* file from the command line in JupyterLab.

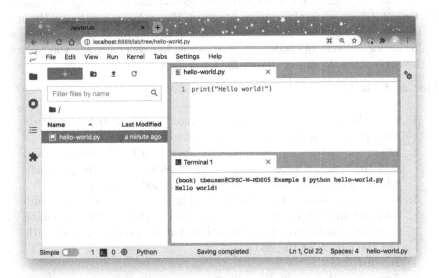

FIGURE 2.3: Executing a simple Python file called hello-world.py from a terminal in JupyterLab.

We recommend you take a look at the JupyterLab documentation[26] to learn more about how to use Jupyterlab. In particular, we'll note that, like VS Code, JupyterLab supports an ecosystem of extensions that can add additional functionality to the IDE. We won't install any here, but you can browse them in the JupyterLab *Extension Manager* if you're interested.

---

[26]https://jupyterlab.readthedocs.io/en/stable/index.html

2.5.3 RStudio

Users with an R background may prefer to stay in the RStudio IDE. We recommend installing the most recent version of the IDE from the RStudio website[27] (we recommend installing at least version ^1.4) and then installing the most recent version of R from CRAN[28]. To use Python in RStudio, you will need to install the reticulate[29] R package by typing the following in the R console inside RStudio:

```
install.packages("reticulate")
```

When installing reticulate, you may be prompted to install the Anaconda distribution. We already installed the Miniconda distribution of Python in **Section 2.2.1**, so answer "no" to this prompt. Before being able to use Python in RStudio, you will need to configure reticulate. We will briefly describe how to do this for different operating systems below, but we encourage you to look at the reticulate documentation[30] for more help.

Mac and Linux

1. Find the path to the Python interpreter installed with Miniconda by typing which python at the command line.
2. Open (or create) an .Rprofile file in your HOME directory and add the line Sys.setenv(RETICULATE_PYTHON = "path_to_python"), where "path_to_python" is the path identified in step 1.
3. Open (or create) a .bash_profile file in your HOME directory and add the line export PATH="/opt/miniconda3/bin:$PATH", replacing /opt/miniconda3/bin with the path you identified in step 1 but without the python at the end.
4. Restart R.
5. Try using Python in RStudio by running the following in the R console:

```
library(reticulate)
repl_python()
```

Windows

1. Find the path to the Python interpreter installed with Miniconda by opening an Anaconda Prompt from the Start Menu and typing where python in a terminal.

---

[27]https://rstudio.com/products/rstudio/download/preview/
[28]https://cran.r-project.org/
[29]https://rstudio.github.io/reticulate/
[30]https://rstudio.github.io/reticulate/

2. Open (or create) an .Rprofile file in your HOME directory and add the line Sys.setenv(RETICULATE_PYTHON = "path_to_python"), where "path_to_python" is the path identified in step 1. Note that in Windows, you need \\ instead of \ to separate the directories; for example your path might look like: C:\\Users\\miniconda3\\python.exe.

3. Open (or create) a .bash_profile file in your HOME directory and add the line export PATH="/opt/miniconda3/bin:$PATH", replacing /opt/miniconda3/bin with the path you identified in step 1 but without the python at the end.

4. Restart R.

5. Try using Python in RStudio by running the following in the R console:

```
library(reticulate)
repl_python()
```

Fig. 2.4 shows an example of executing Python code interactively within the RStudio console.

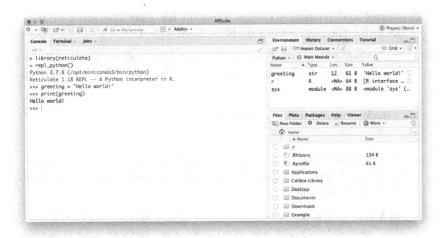

FIGURE 2.4: Executing Python code in the RStudio.

2.6 Developing with Docker

If you have issues installing or using any of the software in this book on your specific operating system, or would prefer to use Docker to help develop your

Python packages, we have provided an alternative software setup with Docker that has everything you need already installed to get started. Docker[31] is a platform that allows you to run and develop software in an isolated environment called a *container*. *Images* contain the instructions required to create a container.

We have developed Docker images to support Python package development in Visual Studio Code or JupyterLab, and we describe minimal workflows for using these images to follow along with this book in the sections below. Feel free to customize these images and/or workflows to suit your specific use cases. We will continue to maintain the Docker images via their GitHub repositories (py-pkgs/docker-vscode[32] and py-pkgs/docker-jupyter[33]) to support readers of this book into the future.

2.6.1   Docker with Visual Studio Code

To develop with Docker inside Visual Studio Code, you can consult the Visual Studio Code official container tutorial[34], or try following the steps below:

1. Install Visual Studio Code from the official website[35].

2. Install and configure Docker Desktop for your operating system following the instructions on the official website[36].

3. Once docker is installed, open a command-line interface and pull the `pypkgs/vscode` docker image by running the following command:

    ```
    $ docker pull pypkgs/vscode
    ```

4. From Visual Studio Code, open/create the working directory you want to develop in (this can be called anything and located wherever you like on your file system).

5. In Visual Studio Code, open the *Extensions* tab on the Visual Studio Code activity bar and search for the "Remote - Containers" extension in the search bar. Install this extension if it is not already installed.

6. Create a file called *.devcontainer.json* in your current working directory (be sure to include the period at the beginning of the file

---

[31]https://docs.docker.com/get-started/overview/

[32]https://github.com/py-pkgs/docker-vscode

[33]https://github.com/py-pkgs/docker-jupyter

[34]https://code.visualstudio.com/docs/remote/containers-tutorial

[35]https://code.visualstudio.com/

[36]https://www.docker.com/get-started

name). This file will tell Visual Studio Code how to run in a Docker container. You can read more about this configuration in the official documentation[37], but for now, a minimal set up requires adding the following content to that file:

```
{
    "name": "poetry",
    "image": "pypkgs/vscode",
    "extensions": ["ms-python.python"],
}
```

7. Now, open the Visual Studio Code Command Palette[38] and search for and select the command "Remote-Containers: Reopen in Container". This command will open Visual Studio Code inside a container made using the pypkgs/vscode Docker image. After Visual Studio Code finishes opening in the container, test that you have access to the three pre-installed pieces of packaging software we need by opening the integrated terminal[39] and trying the following commands:

```
$ poetry --version
$ conda --version
$ cookiecutter --version
```

8. Your development environment is now set up, and you can work with Visual Studio Code as if everything were running locally on your machine (except now your development environment exists inside a container). If you exit Visual Studio Code, your container will stop but will persist on your machine. It can be re-opened at a later time using the "Remote-Containers: Reopen in Container" command we used in step 7.

9. If you want to completely remove your development container to free up memory on your machine, first find the container's ID:

```
$ docker ps -a
```

---

[37] https://code.visualstudio.com/docs/remote/create-dev-container
[38] https://code.visualstudio.com/docs/getstarted/userinterface#_command-palette
[39] https://code.visualstudio.com/docs/editor/integrated-terminal

```
CONTAINER ID    IMAGE
762bca6eb51e    pypkgs/vscode
```

10. Then use the `docker rm` command combined with the container's ID. This will remove the container, including any packages or virtual environments installed in it. However, any files and directories you created will persist on your machine.

```
$ docker rm 762bca6eb51e
```

2.6.2 Docker with JupyterLab

To develop with Docker in JupyterLab follow the instructions below. Helpful information and tutorials can also be found in the Jupyter Docker Stacks documentation[40].

1. Install and configure Docker Desktop for your operating system following the instructions on the official website[41].

2. Once Docker has been installed, open a command-line interface and pull the `pypkgs/jupyter` Docker image by running the `docker pull` command as follows:

```
$ docker pull pypkgs/jupyter
```

3. From the command line, navigate to the directory you want to develop in (this can be called anything and located wherever you like on your file system).

4. Start a new container from that directory by running the following command from the command line:

```
$ docker run -p 8888:8888 \
  -v "${PWD}":/home/jovyan/work \
  pypkgs/jupyter
```

---

[40]https://jupyter-docker-stacks.readthedocs.io/en/latest/index.html
[41]https://www.docker.com/get-started

In the command above, -p binds port 8888 in the container to port 8888 on the host machine and -v mounts the current directory into the container at the location /home/jovyan/work. Windows users that run into issues with the command above may need to try double-slashes in the volume mount path, for example: -v /$(pwd)://home//jovyan//work. You can read more about the docker run command and its arguments in the Docker command-line interface documentation[42].

5. Copy the unique URL printed to screen (that looks something like this: http://127.0.0.1:8888/lab?token=45d53a348580b3acfafa) to your browser. This will open an instance of JupyterLab running inside a Docker container.

6. Navigate to the work directory in JupyterLab. This is where you can develop and create new files and directories that will persist in the directory from where you launched your container.

7. Test that you have access to the three pre-installed pieces of packaging software we need by opening a terminal in JupyterLab and trying the following commands:

```
$ poetry --version
$ conda --version
$ cookiecutter --version
```

8. When you've finished a working session, you can exit JupyterLab, and kill your terminal, and your container will persist. You can restart the container and launch JupyterLab again by first finding its ID:

```
$ docker ps -a
```

```
CONTAINER ID    IMAGE
653daa2cd48e    pypkgs/jupyter
```

9. Then, to restart the container and launch JupyterLab, use the docker start -a command combined with the container's ID:

---

[42]https://docs.docker.com/engine/reference/commandline/run/

```
$ docker start -a 653daa2cd48e
```

10. If you want to completely remove the container you can use the
    docker rm command. This will remove the container, including any
    packages or virtual environments installed in it. However, all files
    and directories added to the work directory will persist on your
    machine.

```
$ docker rm 653daa2cd48e
```

3

How to package a Python

In this chapter we will develop an entire example Python package from beginning-to-end to demonstrate the key steps involved in developing a package. This chapter forms the foundation of this book. It contains everything you need to know to create a Python package and can be used as a reference sheet when creating packages in the future. Later chapters explore each of the individual steps in the packaging process in further detail.

The example package we are going to create in this chapter will help us calculate word counts from a text file. We'll be calling it pycounts, and it will be useful for calculating word usage in texts such as novels, research papers, news articles, log files, and more.

3.1 Counting words in a text file

3.1.1 Developing our code

Before even thinking about making a package, we'll first develop the code we want to package up. The pycounts package we are going to create will help us calculate word counts from a text file. Python has a useful Counter object that can be used to calculate counts of a collection of elements (like a list of words) and store them in a dictionary.

We can demonstrate the functionality of Counter by first opening up a Python interpreter by typing python at the command line:

```
$ python
```

We can then import the Counter class from the collections module:

```
>>> from collections import Counter
```

Now we will define and use a sample list of words to create a Counter object:

DOI: 10.1201/9781003189251-3

```
>>> words = ["a", "happy", "hello", "a", "world", "happy"]
>>> word_counts = Counter(words)
>>> word_counts
```

```
Counter({'a': 2, 'happy': 2, 'hello': 1, 'world': 1})
```

Note how the Counter object automatically calculated the count of each unique word in our input list and returned the result as a dictionary of 'word': count pairs! Given this functionality, how can we use Counter to count the words in a text file? Well, we would need to load the file with Python, split it up into a list of words, and then create a Counter object from that list of words.

We first need a text file to help us build this workflow. "The Zen of Python[1]" is a list of nineteen aphorisms about the Python programming language, which can be viewed by running import this in a Python interpreter:

```
>>> import this
```

```
The Zen of Python, by Tim Peters

Beautiful is better than ugly.
Explicit is better than implicit.
Simple is better than complex.
...
```

Let's make a text file called *zen.txt* containing the "The Zen of Python" text above. Do this by manually copying the above output into a file in your current directory called *zen.txt* using an editor of your choice, or by running the following command at the command line:

```
$ python -c "import this" > zen.txt
```

> In the command above, the -c option allows you to pass a string for Python to execute, and the > directs the output of the command to a file (which in our case is called "zen.txt" and is located in the current directory).

---

[1]https://www.python.org/dev/peps/pep-0020/

Now that we have a text file to work with, we can go back to developing our word-counting workflow. To open *zen.txt* in Python, we can use the open() function to open the file and then the .read() method to read its contents as a Python string. The code below, run in a Python interpreter, saves the contents of *zen.txt* as a string in the variable text:

```
>>> with open("zen.txt") as file:
        text = file.read()
```

Let's see what text looks like:

```
>>> text
```

```
"The Zen of Python, by Tim Peters\n\nBeautiful is better
than ugly.\nExplicit is better than implicit.\nSimple is
better than complex.\nComplex is better than complicated
..."
```

We can see that the text variable is a single string, with the \n symbols indicating a new line in the string.

Before we split the above text into individual words for counting with Counter, we should lowercase all the letters and remove punctuation so that if the same word occurs multiple times with different capitalization or punctuation, it isn't treated as different words by Counter. For example we want "Better", "better", and "better!" to result in three counts of the word "better".

To lowercase all letters in a Python string, we can use the .lower() method:

```
>>> text = text.lower()
```

To remove punctuation, we can find them in our string and replace them with nothing using the .replace() method. Python provides a collection of common punctuation marks in the string module:

```
>>> from string import punctuation
>>> punctuation
```

```
'!"#$%&\'()*+,-./:;<=>?@[\\]^_`{|}~'
```

We can use a for loop to remove each of the above punctuation marks from our text variable by replacing it with nothing, i.e., an empty string (""):

```
>>> for p in punctuation:
        text = text.replace(p, "")
```

With punctuation removed and the letters in text all lowercase, we can now split it up into individual words using the .split() method. This method splits a string into a list of strings using spaces, newlines (\n), and tabs (\t) as separators:

```
>>> words = text.split()
>>> words
```

```
['the', 'zen', 'of', 'python', 'by', 'tim', 'peters',
'beautiful', 'is', 'better', 'than', 'ugly', ...]
```

We've managed to load, pre-process, and split our *zen.txt* file up into individual words and can now determine the word counts by creating a Counter object:

```
>>> from collections import Counter
>>> word_counts = Counter(words)
>>> word_counts
```

```
Counter({'is': 10, 'better': 8, 'than': 8, 'the': 6,
'to': 5, 'of': 3, 'although': 3, 'never': 3, ... })
```

3.1.2   Turning our code into functions

In **Section 3.1.1** we developed a workflow for counting words in a text file. But it would be a pain to run all that code every time we want to count the words in a file! To make things more efficient, let's turn the above code into three reusable functions called load_text(), clean_text(), and count_words() by defining them in our Python interpreter:

We've added a short documentation string (docstring) to each function here using triple quotes. We'll talk more about docstrings in **Section 3.8.2**.

```
>>> def load_text(input_file):
        """Load text from a text file and return as a string."""
        with open(input_file, "r") as file:
            text = file.read()
        return text
```

```
>>> def clean_text(text):
        """Lowercase and remove punctuation from a string."""
        text = text.lower()
        for p in punctuation:
            text = text.replace(p, "")
        return text
```

```
>>> def count_words(input_file):
        """Count unique words in a string."""
        text = load_text(input_file)
        text = clean_text(text)
        words = text.split()
        return Counter(words)
```

We can now use our word-counting functionality as follows:

```
>>> count_words("zen.txt")
```

```
Counter({'is': 10, 'better': 8, 'than': 8, 'the': 6,
'to': 5, 'of': 3, 'although': 3, 'never': 3, ... })
```

Unfortunately, if you quit from the Python interpreter, the functions we just defined will be lost and you will have to define them again in new sessions.

The whole idea of a Python package is that we can store Python code, like our load_text(), clean_text(), and count_words() functions, in a package that we, and others, can install, import, and use at any time and in any project. In the remainder of this chapter, we'll work towards packaging up the code we've written into a Python package called pycounts.

3.2   Package structure

3.2.1   A brief introduction

To develop our pycounts package we first need to create an appropriate directory structure. Python packages consist of a specific directory structure typically including the following:

- A root directory with the name of the package, e.g., *pycounts/*;
- One or more Python modules (files with a *.py* extension that contain Python code) in a subdirectroy *src/pycounts/*;
- Instructions on how to build and install the package on a computer in a file called *pyproject.toml*;
- Important documentation such as a README in the root directory, and additional documentation in a *docs/* subdirectory; and,
- Tests in a *tests/* subdirectory.

An example structure for a package called "pycounts" with two modules ("moduleA" and "moduleB") is shown below. There's a lot of files here, but don't worry; packages are usually created from pre-made templates, as we'll show in the next section. At this point, we're just getting a bird's-eye view of package structure. We'll create and explore each element in this structure as we make our way through this chapter.

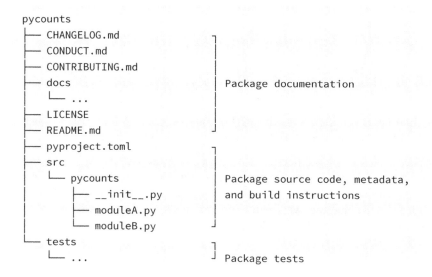

```
pycounts
├── CHANGELOG.md
├── CONDUCT.md
├── CONTRIBUTING.md
├── docs                         Package documentation
│   └── ...
├── LICENSE
├── README.md
├── pyproject.toml
├── src
│   └── pycounts                 Package source code, metadata,
│       ├── __init__.py          and build instructions
│       ├── moduleA.py
│       └── moduleB.py
└── tests
    └── ...                      Package tests
```

It might be confusing to see two directories with the package's name (the root directory pycounts/ and the subdirectory src/pycounts/, but this is how Python packages are typically set up. We'll explore this structure more in the rest of this chapter and discuss it in detail in **Chapter 4: Package structure and distribution.**

3.2.2 Creating a package structure

Most developers use a pre-made template to set up the directory structure of a Python package. We will use the cookiecutter tool (which we installed in **Section 2.2.2**) to create our package structure for us.

cookiecutter is a tool for populating a directory structure from a pre-made template. People have developed and open-sourced many cookiecutter templates for different projects, such as for creating Python packages, R packages, websites, and more. You can find these templates by, for example, searching an online hosting service like GitHub[2]. We have developed our own py-pkgs-cookiecutter Python package template to support this book; it is hosted on GitHub[3].

To use this template to create a package directory structure, you can navigate to the directory where you want to create your package from the command line, and then run the command below. Upon executing this command you will be prompted to provide information that will be used to create your package file and directory structure. We provide an example of how to respond to these prompts below and an explanation of what they mean in Table 3.1.

```
$ cookiecutter https://github.com/py-pkgs/py-pkgs-cookiecutter.git
```

```
author_name [Monty Python]: Tomas Beuzen
package_name [mypkg]: pycounts
package_short_description []: Calculate word counts in a text file!
package_version [0.1.0]:
python_version [3.9]:
Select open_source_license:
1 - MIT
2 - Apache License 2.0
```

---

[2]https://www.github.com
[3]https://github.com/py-pkgs/py-pkgs-cookiecutter

```
3 - GNU General Public License v3.0
4 - Creative Commons Attribution 4.0
5 - BSD 3-Clause
6 - Proprietary
7 - None
Choose from 1, 2, 3, 4, 5, 6 [1]:
Select include_github_actions:
1 - no
2 - ci
3 - ci+cd
Choose from 1, 2, 3 [1]:
```

TABLE 3.1: A description of the py-pkgs-cookiecutter template prompts.

Prompt keyword	Description
author_name, package_name, package_short_description	These are self-explanatory. Note that we will be publishing our pycounts package to Python's main package index PyPI, where names must be unique. **If you plan to follow along with this tutorial you should choose a unique name for your package.** Something like pycounts_[your intials] might be appropriate, but you can check if a name is already taken by searching for it on PyPI. We provide guidance on choosing a good package name in **Section 4.2.2**.
package_version	The version of your package. Most packages use semantic versioning, where a version number consists of three integers A.B.C. A is the "major" version, B is the "minor" version, and C is the "patch" version. The first version of a package usually starts at 0.1.0 and increments from there. We'll discuss versioning in **Chapter 7: Releasing and versioning**.
python_version	The minimum version of Python your package will support. We'll talk more about versions and constraints in **Section 3.6.1**

Prompt keyword	Description
open_source_license	The license that dictates how your package can be used by others. We discuss licenses in **Section 6.2.2**. The MIT license we chose in our example is a permissive license commonly used for open-source work. If your project will not be open source you can choose not to include a license.
include_github_actions	An option to include continuous integration and continuous deployment files for use with GitHub Actions. We'll explore these topics in **Chapter 8: Continuous integration and deployment,** so for now, we recommend responding no.

After responding to the `py-pkgs-cookiecutter` prompts, we have a new directory called `pycounts`, full of content suitable for building a fully-featured Python package! We'll explore each element of this directory structure as we develop our `pycounts` package throughout this chapter.

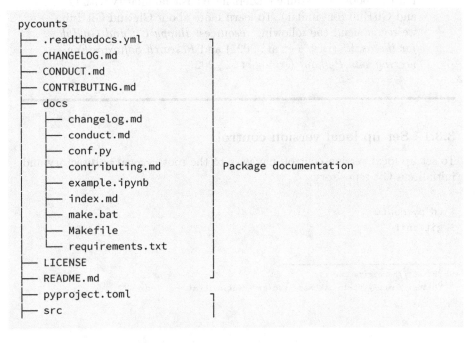

```
pycounts
├── .readthedocs.yml
├── CHANGELOG.md
├── CONDUCT.md
├── CONTRIBUTING.md
├── docs
│   ├── changelog.md
│   ├── conduct.md
│   ├── conf.py
│   ├── contributing.md          Package documentation
│   ├── example.ipynb
│   ├── index.md
│   ├── make.bat
│   ├── Makefile
│   └── requirements.txt
├── LICENSE
├── README.md
├── pyproject.toml
├── src
```

```
|   └── pycounts            | Package source code, metadata,
|       ├── __init__.py     | and build instructions
|       └── pycounts.py     ┘
└── tests                   ┐
    └── test_pycounts.py    ┘ Package tests
```

3.3   Put your package under version control

Before continuing to develop our package it is good practice to put it under local and remote version control. This is not necessary for developing a package, but it is highly recommended so that you can better manage and track changes to your package over time. Version control is particularly useful if you plan on collaborating on your package with others. If you don't want to use version control, feel free to skip to **Section 3.4**. The tools we will be using for version control in this book are Git and GitHub (which we set up in **Section 2.4**).

For this book, we assume readers have basic familiarity with Git and GitHub (or similar). To learn more about Git and GitHub, we recommend the following resources: *Happy Git and GitHub for the useR*[4] (Bryan et al., 2021) and *Research Software Engineering with Python*[5] (Irving et al., 2021).

3.3.1   Set up local version control

To set up local version control, navigate to the root *pycounts/* directory and initialize a Git repository:

```
$ cd pycounts
$ git init
```

---

[4]https://happygitwithr.com
[5]https://merely-useful.tech/py-rse/git-cmdline.html

```
Initialized empty Git repository in /Users/tomasbeuzen/pycounts/.git/
```

Next, we need to tell Git which files to track for version control (which will be all of them at this point) and then commit these changes locally:

```
$ git add .
$ git commit -m "initial package setup"
```

```
[master (root-commit) 51795ad] initial package setup
 20 files changed, 502 insertions(+)
 create mode 100644 .gitignore
 create mode 100644 .readthedocs.yml
 create mode 100644 CHANGELOG.md
 ...
 create mode 100644 src/pycounts/__init__.py
 create mode 100644 src/pycounts/pycounts.py
 create mode 100644 tests/test_pycounts.py
```

3.3.2 Set up remote version control

Now that we have set up local version control, we will create a repository on GitHub[6] and set that as the remote version control home for this project. First, we need to create a new repository on GitHub[7] as demonstrated in Fig. 3.1:

Next, select the following options when setting up your GitHub repository, as shown in Fig. 3.2:

1. Give the GitHub repository the same name as your Python package and give it a short description.
2. You can choose to make your repository public or private — we'll be making ours public so we can share it with others.
3. Do not initialize the repository with any files (we've already created all our files locally using the `py-pkgs-cookiecutter` template).

Now, use the commands shown on GitHub, and outlined in Fig. 3.3, to link your local and remote repositories and push your local content to GitHub:

---

[6]https://github.com/
[7]https://www.github.com

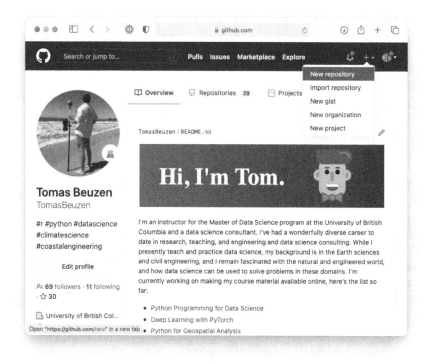

FIGURE 3.1: Creating a new repository in GitHub.

The commands below should be specific to your GitHub username and the name of your Python package. They use SSH
authentication to connect to GitHub which you will need to set
up by following the steps in the official GitHub documentation[8].

```
$ git remote add origin git@github.com:TomasBeuzen/pycounts.git
$ git branch -M main
$ git push -u origin main
```

---

[8]https://docs.github.com/en/authentication/connecting-to-github-with-ssh

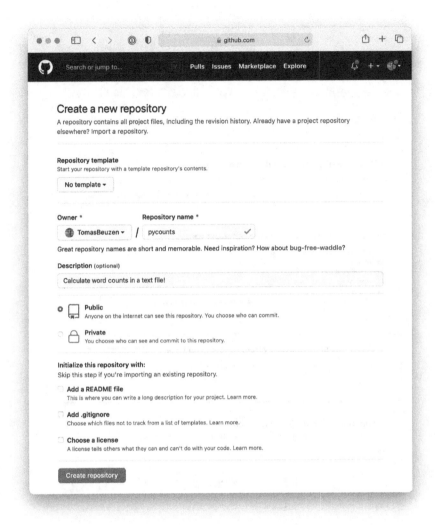

FIGURE 3.2: Setting up a new repository in GitHub.

```
Enumerating objects: 26, done.
Counting objects: 100% (26/26), done.
Delta compression using up to 8 threads
Compressing objects: 100% (19/19), done.
Writing objects: 100% (26/26), 8.03 KiB | 4.01 MiB/s, done.
Total 26 (delta 0), reused 0 (delta 0)
To github.com:TomasBeuzen/pycounts.git
```

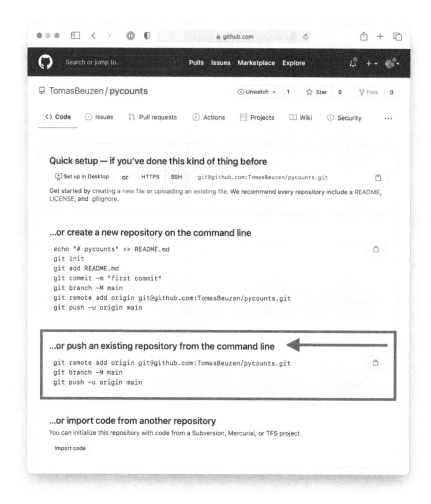

FIGURE 3.3: Instructions on how to link local and remote version control repositories.

```
* [new branch]        main -> main
Branch 'main' set up to track remote branch 'main' from 'origin'.
```

3.4   Packaging your code

We now have our pycounts package structure set up, and are ready to populate our package with the load_text(), clean_text() and count_words() functions we developed at the beginning of the chapter in **Section 3.1.2**. Where should we put these functions? Let's review the structure of our package:

```
pycounts
├── .readthedocs.yml
├── CHANGELOG.md
├── CONDUCT.md
├── CONTRIBUTING.md
├── docs
│   └── ...
├── LICENSE
├── pyproject.toml
├── README.md
├── src
│   └── pycounts
│       ├── __init__.py
│       └── pycounts.py
└── tests
    └── ...
```

The Python code for our package should live in modules in the *src/pycounts/* directory. The py-pkgs-cookiecutter template already created a Python module for us to put our code in called *src/pycounts/pycounts.py* (note that this module can be named anything, but it is common for a module to share the name of the package). We'll copy the functions we created in **Section 3.1.2** to the module *src/pycounts/pycounts.py* now. Our functions depends on collections.Counter and string.punctuation, so we also need to import those at the top of the file. Here's what *src/pycounts/pycounts.py* should now look like:

```python
from collections import Counter
from string import punctuation

def load_text(input_file):
    """Load text from a text file and return as a string."""
    with open(input_file, "r") as file:
        text = file.read()
    return text

def clean_text(text):
    """Lowercase and remove punctuation from a string."""
    text = text.lower()
    for p in punctuation:
        text = text.replace(p, "")
```

```
    return text

def count_words(input_file):
    """Count unique words in a string."""
    text = load_text(input_file)
    text = clean_text(text)
    words = text.split()
    return Counter(words)
```

3.5 Test drive your package code

3.5.1 Create a virtual environment

Before we install and test our package, it is highly recommended to set up a virtual environment. As discussed previously in **Section 2.2.1**, a virtual environment provides a safe and isolated space to develop and install packages. If you don't want to use a virtual environment, feel free to skip to **Section 3.5.2**.

There are several options available when it comes to creating and managing virtual environments (e.g., conda or venv). We will use conda (which we installed in **Section 2.2.1**) because it is a simple, commonly used, and effective tool for managing virtual environments.

To use conda to create a new virtual environment called pycounts that contains Python, run the following in your terminal:

```
$ conda create --name pycounts python=3.9 -y
```

We are specifying python=3.9 because that is the minimum version of Python we specified that our package will support in **Section 3.2.2**.

To use this new environment for developing and installing software we need to "activate" it:

```
$ conda activate pycounts
```

In most command lines, `conda` will add a prefix like (`pycounts`) to your command-line prompt to indicate which environment you are working in. Any-time you wish to work on your package, you should activate its virtual environment. You can view the packages currently installed in a `conda` environment using the command `conda list`, and you can exit a `conda` virtual environment using `conda deactivate`.

---

poetry, the packaging tool we'll use to develop our package later in this chapter, also supports virtual environment management[9] without the need for `conda`. However, we find `conda` to be a more intuitive and explicit environment manager, which is why we advocate for it in this book.

3.5.2 Installing your package

We have our package structure set up and we've populated it with our Python code. How do we install and use our package? There are several tools available to develop installable Python packages. The most common are `poetry`, `flit`, and `setuptools`, which we compare in **Section 4.3.3**. In this book, we will be using `poetry` (which we installed in **Section 2.2.2**); it is a modern packaging tool that provides simple and efficient commands to develop, install, and distribute Python packages.

In a poetry-managed package, the *pyproject.toml* file stores all the metadata and install instructions for the package. The *pyproject.toml* that the py-pkgs-cookiecutter created for our pycounts package looks like this:

```
[tool.poetry]
name = "pycounts"
version = "0.1.0"
description = "Calculate word counts in a text file."
authors = ["Tomas Beuzen"]
license = "MIT"
readme = "README.md"
```

---

[9]https://python-poetry.org/docs/managing-environments/

```
[tool.poetry.dependencies]
python = "^3.9"

[tool.poetry.dev-dependencies]

[build-system]
requires = ["poetry-core>=1.0.0"]
build-backend = "poetry.core.masonry.api"
```

Table 3.2 provides a brief description of each of the headings in that file (called "tables" in TOML file jargon).

TABLE 3.2: A description of the tables in the pyproject.toml.

TOML table	Description
[tool.poetry]	Defines package metadata. The name, version, description, and authors of the package are required.
[tool.poetry.dependencies]	Identifies dependencies of a package — that is, software that the package depends on. Our pycounts package only depends on Python 3.9 or higher, but we'll add other dependencies to our package later in this chapter.
[tool.poetry.dev-dependencies]	Identifies development dependencies of a package — dependencies required for development purposes, such as running tests or building documentation. We'll add development dependencies to our pycounts package later in this chapter.
[build-system]	Identifies the build tools required to build your package. We'll talk more about this in **Section 3.10**.

With our *pyproject.toml* file already set up for us by the py-pkgs-cookiecutter template, we can use poetry to install our package using the command poetry install at the command line from the root package directory:

```
$ poetry install
```

```
Updating dependencies
Resolving dependencies... (0.1s)
```

```
Writing lock file
```

```
Installing the current project: pycounts (0.1.0)
```

When you run `poetry install`, poetry creates a *poetry.lock* file, which contains a record of all the dependencies you've installed while developing your package. For anyone else working on your project (including you in the future), running `poetry install` installs dependencies from *poetry.lock* to ensure that they have the same versions of dependencies that you did when developing the package. We won't be focusing on *poetry.lock* in this book, but it can be a helpful development tool, which you can read more about in the `poetry` documentation[10].

With our package installed, we can now `import` and use it in a Python session. Before we do that, we need a text file to test our package on. Feel free to use any text file, but we'll create the same "Zen of Python" text file we used earlier in the chapter by running the following at the command line:

```
$ python -c "import this" > zen.txt
```

Now we can open a Python interpreter and `import` and use the `count_words()` function from our `pycounts` module with the following code:

```
>>> from pycounts.pycounts import count_words
>>> count_words("zen.txt")
```

```
Counter({'is': 10, 'better': 8, 'than': 8, 'the': 6,
'to': 5, 'of': 3, 'although': 3, 'never': 3, ... })
```

---

[10]https://python-poetry.org/docs/basic-usage/#installing-dependencies

Looks like everything is working! We have now created and installed a simple Python package! You can now use this Python package in any project you wish (if using virtual environments, you'll need to `poetry install` the package in them before it can be used).

`poetry install` actually installs packages in "editable mode", which means that it installs a link to your package's code on your computer (rather than installing it as a independent piece of software). Editable installs are commonly used by developers because it means that any edits made to the package's source code are immediately available the next time it is imported, without having to `poetry install` again. We'll talk more about installing packages in **Section 3.10**.

In the next section, we'll show how to add code to our package that depends on another package. But for those using version control, it's a good idea to commit the changes we've made to *src/pycounts/pycounts.py* to local and remote version control:

```
$ git add src/pycounts/pycounts.py
$ git commit -m "feat: add word counting functions"
$ git push
```

> In this book, we use the Angular style[11] for Git commit messages. We'll talk about this style more in **Section 7.2.2**, but our commit messages have the form "type: subject", where "type" indicates the kind of change being made and "subject" contains a description of the change. We'll be using the following "types" for our commits:

- "build": indicates a change to the build system or external dependencies.
- "docs": indicates a change to documentation.
- "feat": indicates a new feature being added to the code base.
- "fix": indicates a bug fix.
- "test": indicates changes to testing framework.

---

[11]https://github.com/angular/angular.js/blob/master/DEVELOPERS.md#-git-commit-guidelines

3.6 Adding dependencies to your package

Let's now add a new function to our package that can plot a bar chart of the top n words in a Counter object of word counts. Imagine we've come up with the following plot_words() function that does this. The function uses the convenient .most_common() method of the Counter object to return a list of tuples of the top n words counts in the format (word, count). It then uses the Python function zip(*...) to unpack that list of tuples into two individual lists, word and count. Finally, the matplotlib (Hunter, 2007) package is used to plot the result (plt.bar(...)), which looks like Fig. 3.4.

If this code is not familiar to you, don't worry! The code itself is not overly important to our discussion of packaging. You just need to know that we are adding some new code to our package that depends on the matplotlib package.

```python
import matplotlib.pyplot as plt

def plot_words(word_counts, n=10):
    """Plot a bar chart of word counts."""
    top_n_words = word_counts.most_common(n)
    word, count = zip(*top_n_words)
    fig = plt.bar(range(n), count)
    plt.xticks(range(n), labels=word, rotation=45)
    plt.xlabel("Word")
    plt.ylabel("Count")
    return fig
```

Where should we put this function in our package? You could certainly add all your package code into a single module (e.g., *src/pycounts/pycounts.py*), but as you add functionality to your package that module will quickly become overcrowded and hard to manage. Instead, as you write more code, it's a good idea to organize it into multiple, logical modules. With that in mind, we'll create a new module called *src/pycounts/plotting.py* to house our plotting function plot_words(). Create that new module now in an editor of your choice.

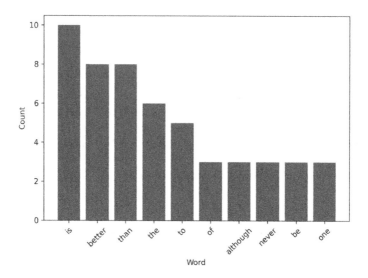

FIGURE 3.4: Example figure created from the plotting function.

Your package structure should now look like this:

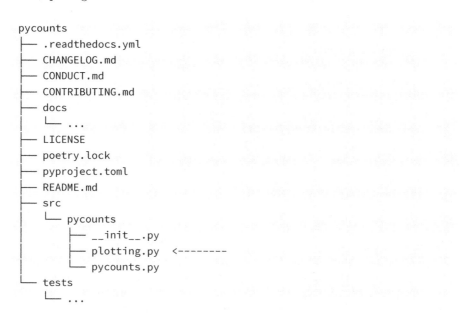

Open *src/pycounts/plotting.py* and add the `plot_words()` code from above (don't forget to add the `import matplotlib.pyplot as plt` at the top of the module).

After doing this, if we tried to import our new function in a Python interpreter we'd get an error:

If using a conda virtual environment, make sure that environment is active by running conda activate pycounts, before using or working on your package.

```
>>> from pycounts.plotting import plot_words
```

```
ModuleNotFoundError: No module named 'matplotlib'
```

This is because matplotlib is not part of the standard Python library; we need to install it and add it as a dependency of our pycounts package. We can do this with poetry using the command poetry add. This command will install the specified dependency into the current virtual environment and will update the [tool.poetry.dependencies] section of the *pyproject.toml* file:

```
$ poetry add matplotlib
```

```
Using version ^3.4.3 for matplotlib

Updating dependencies
Resolving dependencies...

Writing lock file

Package operations: 8 installs, 0 updates, 0 removals

  • Installing six (1.16.0)
  • Installing cycler (0.10.0)
  • Installing kiwisolver (1.3.1)
  • Installing numpy (1.21.1)
  • Installing pillow (8.3.1)
  • Installing pyparsing (2.4.7)
  • Installing python-dateutil (2.8.2)
  • Installing matplotlib (3.4.3)
```

If you open *pyproject.toml* file, you should now see `matplotlib` listed as a dependency under the `[tool.poetry.dependencies]` section (which previously only contained Python 3.9 as a dependency, as we saw in **Section 3.5.2**):

```
[tool.poetry.dependencies]
python = "^3.9"
matplotlib = "^3.4.3"
```

We can now use our package in a Python interpreter as follows (be sure that the *zen.txt* file we created earlier is in the current directory if you're running the code below):

```
>>> from pycounts.pycounts import count_words
>>> from pycounts.plotting import plot_words
>>> counts = count_words("zen.txt")
>>> fig = plot_words(counts, 10)
```

If running the above Python code in an interactive IPython shell or Jupyter Notebook, the plot will be displayed automatically. If you're running from the Python interpreter, you'll need to run the `matplotlib` command `plt.show()` to display the plot, as shown below:

```
>>> import matplotlib.pyplot as plt
>>> plt.show()
```

We've made some important changes to our package in this section by adding a new module and a dependency. Those using version control should commit these changes:

```
$ git add src/pycounts/plotting.py
$ git commit -m "feat: add plotting module"
$ git add pyproject.toml poetry.lock
$ git commit -m "build: add matplotlib as a dependency"
$ git push
```

3.6.1 Dependency version constraints

Versioning is the practice of assigning a unique identifier to unique releases of a package. For example, semantic versioning[12] is a common versioning system that consists of three integers A.B.C. A is the "major" version, B is the "minor" version, and C is the "patch" version identifier. Package versions usually starts

---

[12]https://semver.org

at 0.1.0 and positively increment the major, minor, and patch numbers from there, depending on the kind of changes made to the package over time.

We'll talk more about versioning in **Chapter 7: Releasing and versioning**, but what's important to know now is that we typically constrain the required version number(s) of our package's dependencies, to ensure we're using versions that are up-to-date and contain the functionality we need. You may have noticed `poetry` prepended a caret (^) operator to the dependency versions in our *pyproject.toml* file, under the [tool.poetry.dependencies] section:

```
[tool.poetry.dependencies]
python = "^3.9"
matplotlib = "^3.4.3"
```

The caret operator is short-hand for "requires this or any higher version that does not modify the left-most non-zero version digit". For example, our package depends on any Python version >=3.9.0 and <4.0.0. Thus, examples of valid versions include 3.9.1 and 3.12.0, but 4.0.1 would be invalid. There are many other syntaxes that can be used to specify version constraints in different ways, as you can read more about in the `poetry` documentation[13]. So why do we care about this? The caret operator enforces an upper cap on the dependency versions our package requires. A problem with this approach is that it forces anyone depending on your package to specify the same constraints and can thus make it difficult to add and resolve dependencies.

This problem is best shown by example. Version 1.21.5 of the popular `numpy` (Harris et al., 2020) package had bound version constraints on Python, requiring version >=3.7 and <3.11 (see the source code[14]). Watch what happens if we try to add this version of `numpy` to our `pycounts` package (we use the argument `--dry-run` to show what would happen here without actually executing anything):

```
$ poetry add numpy=1.21.5 --dry-run


Updating dependencies
Resolving dependencies... (0.1s)

SolverProblemError

The current project's Python requirement (>=3.9,<4.0) is not compatible
with some of the required packages Python requirement:
```

---

[13]https://python-poetry.org/docs/dependency-specification
[14]https://github.com/numpy/numpy/blob/c3d0a09342c08c466984654bc4738af595fba896/setup.py#L409

```
-  numpy requires Python >=3.7,<3.11, so it will not be satisfied
   for Python >=3.11,<4.0
```

The problem here is that our package currently supports Python versions ^3.9
(i.e., >=3.9.0 and <4.0.0), so if we released it, a user with Python 3.12.0 would
technically be able to install it. However, numpy 1.21.5 only supports >=3.7
and <3.11 which would not be compatible with Python 3.12.0 (or any version
>=3.11). As a result of this inconsistency, poetry refuses to add numpy 1.21.5
as a dependency of our package. To add it, we have three main choices:

1. Change the Python version constraints of our package to >=3.7
   and <3.11.
2. Wait for a version of numpy that is compatible with our package's
   Python constraints.
3. Manually specify the versions of Python for which the dependency
   can be installed, e.g.: poetry add numpy=1.21.5 --python ">=3.7,
   <3.11".

None of these options is really ideal, especially if your package has a large
number of dependencies with different bound version constraints. However, a
simple way this issue could be resolved is if numpy 1.21.5 did not having an
upper cap on the Python version required. In fact, in the subsequent minor
version release of numpy, 1.22.0, the upper version cap on Python was removed,
requiring only version >=3.8 (see the source code[15]), which we would be able
to successfully add to our package:

```
$ poetry add numpy=1.22.0 --dry-run
```

Ultimately, version constraints are an important issue that can affect the us-
ability of your package. If you intend to share your package, having an upper
cap on dependency versions can make it very difficult for other developers
to use your package as a dependency in their own projects. At the time of
writing, much of the packaging community, including the Python Packaging
Authority[16], generally recommend not using an upper cap on version constraints unless absolutely necessary. As a result, we recommend specifying
version constraints without an upper cap by manually changing poetry's default caret operator (^) to a greater-than-or-equal-to sign (>=). For example,
we will change the [tool.poetry.dependencies] section of our *pyproject.toml*
file as follows:

---

[15]https://github.com/numpy/numpy/blob/4adc87dff15a247e417d50f10cc4def8e1c17a03/setup
.py#L410
[16]https://github.com/pypa/packaging.python.org/pull/850

```
[tool.poetry.dependencies]
python = ">=3.9"
matplotlib = ">=3.4.3"
```

You can read more about the issues around version constraints, as well as examples where they might actually be valid, in Henry Schreiner's excellent blog post[17]. Those using version control should commit this import change we've made to our package:

```
$ git add pyproject.toml
$ git commit -m "build: remove upper bound on dependency versions"
$ git push
```

3.7 Testing your package

3.7.1 Writing tests

At this point we have developed a package that can count words in a text file and plot the results. But how can we be certain that our package works correctly and produces reliable results?

One thing we can do is write tests for our package that check the package is working as expected. This is particularly important if you intend to share your package with others (you don't want to share code that doesn't work!). But even if you don't intend to share your package, writing tests can still be helpful to catch errors in your code and to write new code without breaking any tried-and-tested existing functionality. If you don't want to write to tests for your package feel free to skip to **Section 3.8**.

Many of us already conduct informal tests of our code by running it a few times in a Python session to see if it's working as we expect, and if not, changing the code and repeating the process. This is called "manual testing" or "exploratory testing". However, when writing software, it's preferable to define your tests in a more formal and reproducible way.

Tests in Python are often written with the assert statement. assert checks the truth of an expression; if the expression is true, Python does nothing and continues running, but if it's false, the code terminates and shows a user-defined error message. For example, consider running the follow code in a Python interpreter:

---

[17]https://iscinumpy.dev/post/bound-version-constraints/

```
>>> ages = [32, 19, 9, 75]
>>> for age in ages:
>>>     assert age >= 18, "Person is younger than 18!"
>>>     print("Age verified!")


Age verified!
Age verified!
Traceback (most recent call last):
  File "<stdin>", line 2, in <module>
AssertionError: Person is younger than 18!
```

Note how the first two "ages" (32 and 19) are verified, with an "Age verified!" message printed to screen. But the third age of 9 fails the assert, so an error message is raised and the program terminates before checking the last age of 75.

Using the assert statement, let's write a test for the count_words() function of our pycounts package. There are different kinds of tests used to test software (unit tests, integration tests, regression tests, etc.); we discuss these in **Chapter 5: Testing**. For now, we'll write a unit test. Unit tests evaluate a single "unit" of software, such as a Python function, to check that it produces an expected result. A unit test consists of:

1. Some data to test the code with (called a "*fixture*"). The fixture is typically a small or simple version of the data the function will typically process.
2. The *actual* result that the code produces given the fixture.
3. The *expected* result of the test, which is compared to the *actual* result using an assert statement.

The unit test we are going to write will assert that the count_words() function produces an expected result given a certain fixture. We'll use the following quote from Albert Einstein as our fixture:

"Insanity is doing the same thing over and over and expecting different results."

The *actual* result is the result count_words() outputs when we input this fixture. We can get the *expected* result by manually counting the words in the quote (ignoring capitalization and punctuation):

```
einstein_counts = {'insanity': 1, 'is': 1, 'doing': 1,
                   'the': 1, 'same': 1, 'thing': 1,
                   'over': 2, 'and': 2, 'expecting': 1,
                   'different': 1, 'results': 1}
```

To write our unit test in Python code, let's first create a text file containing the Einstein quote to use as our fixture. We'll add it to the *tests/* directory of our package as a file called *einstein.txt* — you can make the file manually, or you can create it from a Python session started in the root package directory using the following code:

```
>>> quote = "Insanity is doing the same thing over and over and \
        expecting different results."
>>> with open("tests/einstein.txt", "w") as file:
        file.write(quote)
```

Now, a unit test for our `count_words()` function would look as below:

```
>>> from pycounts.pycounts import count_words
>>> from collections import Counter
>>> expected = Counter({'insanity': 1, 'is': 1, 'doing': 1,
                        'the': 1, 'same': 1, 'thing': 1,
                        'over': 2, 'and': 2, 'expecting': 1,
                        'different': 1, 'results': 1})
>>> actual = count_words("tests/einstein.txt")
>>> assert actual == expected, "Einstein quote counted incorrectly!"
```

If the above code runs without error, our `count_words()` function is working, at least to our test specifications. In the next section, we'll discuss how we can make this testing process more efficient.

3.7.2 Running tests

It would be tedious and inefficient to manually write and execute unit tests for your package's code like we did above. Instead, it's common to use a "testing framework" to automatically run our tests for us. `pytest` is the most common test framework used for Python packages. To use `pytest`:

1. Tests are defined as functions prefixed with `test_` and contain one or more statements that `assert` code produces an expected result.

2. Tests are put in files of the form *test_*.py* or **_test.py*, and are usually placed in a directory called *tests/* in a package's root.
3. Tests can be executed using the command pytest at the command line and pointing it to the directory your tests live in (i.e., pytest tests/). pytest will find all files of the form *test_*.py* or **_test.py* in that directory and its sub-directories, and execute any functions with names prefixed with test_.

The py-pkgs-cookiecutter created a *tests/* directory and a module called *test_pycounts.py* for us to put our tests in:

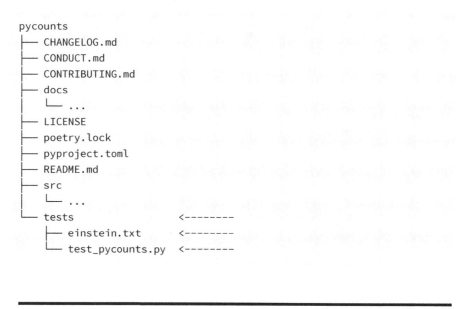

```
pycounts
├── CHANGELOG.md
├── CONDUCT.md
├── CONTRIBUTING.md
├── docs
│   └── ...
├── LICENSE
├── poetry.lock
├── pyproject.toml
├── README.md
├── src
│   └── ...
└── tests                    <--------
    ├── einstein.txt         <--------
    └── test_pycounts.py     <--------
```

We created the file *tests/einstein.txt* ourselves in **Section 3.7.1**, it was not created by the py-pkgs-cookiecutter.

As mentioned above, pytest tests are written as functions prefixed with test_ and which contain one or more assert statements that check some code functionality. Based on this format, let's add the unit test we created in **Section 3.7.1** as a test function to *tests/test_pycounts.py* using the below Python code:

```python
from pycounts.pycounts import count_words
from collections import Counter
```

```python
def test_count_words():
    """Test word counting from a file."""
    expected = Counter({'insanity': 1, 'is': 1, 'doing': 1,
                        'the': 1, 'same': 1, 'thing': 1,
                        'over': 2, 'and': 2, 'expecting': 1,
                        'different': 1, 'results': 1})
    actual = count_words("tests/einstein.txt")
    assert actual == expected, "Einstein quote counted incorrectly!"
```

Before we can use `pytest` to run our test for us we need to add it as a development dependency of our package using the command `poetry add --dev`. A development dependency is a package that is not required by a user to use your package but is required for development purposes (like testing):

If using a `conda` virtual environment, make sure that environment is active by running `conda activate pycounts`, before using or working on your package.

```
$ poetry add --dev pytest
```

If you look in the `pyproject.toml` file you will see that `pytest` gets added under the `[tool.poetry.dev-dependencies]` section (which was previously empty, as we saw in **Section 3.5.2**):

```
[tool.poetry.dev-dependencies]
pytest = "^6.2.5"
```

To use `pytest` to run our test we can use the following command from our root package directory:

```
$ pytest tests/
```

```
========================= test session starts =========================
...
collected 1 item
```

```
tests/test_pycounts.py .                                    [100%]

=========================== 1 passed in 0.01s ===========================
```

> If you're not developing your package in a conda virtual environ-
> ment, poetry will automatically create a virtual environment for
> you using a tool called venv (read more in the documentation[18]).
> You'll need to tell poetry to use this environment by prepending
> any command you run with poetry run, like: poetry run pytest
> tests/.

From the pytest output we can see that our test passed! At this point, we
could add more tests for our package by writing more test_* functions. But
we'll do this in **Chapter 5: Testing**. Typically you want to write enough tests
to check all the core code of your package. We'll show how you can calculate
how much of your package's code your tests actually check in the next section.

3.7.3   Code coverage

A good test suite will contain tests that check as much of your package's code
as possible. How much of your code your tests actually use is called "code
coverage". The simplest and most intuitive measure of code coverage is line
coverage. It is the proportion of lines of your package's code that are executed
by your tests:

$$\text{coverage} = \frac{\text{lines executed}}{\text{total lines}} * 100\%$$

There is a useful extension to pytest called pytest-cov, which we can use to
calculate coverage. First, we'll use poetry to add pytest-cov as a development
dependency of our pycounts package:

```
$ poetry add --dev pytest-cov
```

We can calculate the line coverage of our tests by running the following command, which tells pytest-cov to calculate the coverage our tests have of our
pycounts package:

---

[18]https://python-poetry.org/docs/managing-environments/

```
$ pytest tests/ --cov=pycounts
```

```
========================= test session starts =========================
...

Name                         Stmts   Miss  Cover
----------------------------------------------------
src/pycounts/__init__.py         2      0   100%
src/pycounts/plotting.py         9      9     0%
src/pycounts/pycounts.py        16      0   100%
----------------------------------------------------
TOTAL                           27      9    67%

========================= 1 passed in 0.02s =========================
```

In the output above, Stmts is how many lines are in a module, Miss is how many lines were not executed during your tests, and Cover is the percentage of lines covered by your tests. From the above output, we can see that our tests currently don't cover any of the lines in the pycounts.plotting module. We'll write more tests for our package, and discuss more advanced methods of testing and calculating code coverage in **Chapter 5: Testing**.

For those using version control, commit the changes we've made to our packages tests to local and remote version control:

```
$ git add pyproject.toml poetry.lock
$ git commit -m "build: add pytest and pytest-cov as dev dependencies"
$ git add tests/*
$ git commit -m "test: add unit test for count_words"
$ git push
```

3.8   Package documentation

Documentation describing what your package does and how to use it is invaluable for the users of your package (including yourself). The amount of documentation needed to support a package varies depending on its complexity and the intended audience. A typical package contains documentation in various parts of its directory structure, as shown in Table 3.3. There's a lot here but don't worry, we'll show how to efficiently write all these pieces of documentation in the following sections.

TABLE 3.3: Typical Python package documentation.

Documentation	Typical location	Description
README	Root	Provides high-level information about the package, e.g., what it does, how to install it, and how to use it.
License	Root	Explains who owns the copyright to your package source and how it can be used and shared.
Contributing guidelines	Root	Explains how to contribute to the project.
Code of conduct	Root	Defines standards for how to appropriately engage with and contribute to the project.
Changelog	Root	A chronologically ordered list of notable changes to the package over time, usually organized by version.
Docstrings	*.py* files	Text appearing as the first statement in a function, method, class, or module in Python that describes what the code does and how to use it. Accessible to users via the `help()` command.
Examples	*docs/*	Step-by-step, tutorial-like examples showing how the package works in more detail.

Documentation	Typical location	Description
Application programming interface (API) reference	*docs/*	An organized list of the user-facing functionality of your package (i.e., functions, classes, etc.) along with a short description of what they do and how to use them. Typically created automatically from your package's docstrings using the sphinx tool as we'll discuss in **Section 3.8.4.**

Our pycounts package is a good example of a package with all this documentation:

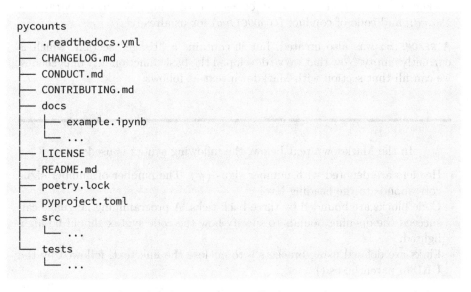

```
pycounts
├── .readthedocs.yml
├── CHANGELOG.md
├── CONDUCT.md
├── CONTRIBUTING.md
├── docs
│   ├── example.ipynb
│   └── ...
├── LICENSE
├── README.md
├── poetry.lock
├── pyproject.toml
├── src
│   └── ...
└── tests
    └── ...
```

The typical workflow for documenting a Python package consists of three steps:

1. **Write documentation**: manually write documentation in a plain-text format.
2. **Build documentation**: compile and render documentation into HTML using the documentation generator sphinx.

3. **Host documentation online**: share the built documentation online so it can be easily accessed by anyone with an internet connection, using a free service like Read the Docs[19] or GitHub Pages[20].

In this section, we will walk through each of these steps in detail.

3.8.1   Writing documentation

Python package documentation is typically written in a plain-text markup format such as Markdown[21] (*.md*) or reStructuredText[22] (*.rst*). With a plain-text
markup language, documents are written in plain-text and a special syntax
is used to specify how the text should be formatted when it is rendered by
a suitable tool. We'll show an example of this below, but we'll be using the
Markdown language in this book because it is widely used, and we feel it has
a less verbose and more intuitive syntax than reStructuredText (check out the
Markdown Guide[23] to learn more about Markdown syntax).

Most developers create packages from templates which pre-populate a lot of
the standard package documentation for them. For example, as we saw in **Section 3.8**, the `py-pkgs-cookiecutter` template we used to create our `pycounts`
package created a *LICENSE*, *CHANGELOG.md*, contributing guidelines (*CONTRIBUT-
ING.md*), and code of conduct (*CONDUCT.md*) for us already!

A *README.md* was also created, but it contains a "Usage" section, which is
currently empty. Now that we've developed the basic functionality of `pycounts`,
we can fill that section with Markdown text as follows:

In the Markdown text below, the following syntax is used:

- Headers are denoted with number signs (#). The number of number signs
  corresponds to the heading level.
- Code blocks are bounded by three back-ticks. A programming language can
  succeed the opening bounds to specify how the code syntax should be highlighted.
- Links are defined using brackets [] to enclose the link text, followed by the
  URL in parentheses ().

---

[19]https://readthedocs.org
[20]https://pages.github.com
[21]https://en.wikipedia.org/wiki/Markdown
[22]https://www.sphinx-doc.org/en/master/usage/restructuredtext/index.html
[23]https://www.markdownguide.org

pycounts

Calculate word counts in a text file!

Installation

```bash
$ pip install pycounts
```

Usage

`pycounts` can be used to count words in a text file and plot results
as follows:

```python
from pycounts.pycounts import count_words
from pycounts.plotting import plot_words
import matplotlib.pyplot as plt

file_path = "test.txt"  # path to your file
counts = count_words(file_path)
fig = plot_words(counts, n=10)
plt.show()
```

Contributing

Interested in contributing? Check out the contributing guidelines.
Please note that this project is released with a Code of Conduct.
By contributing to this project, you agree to abide by its terms.

License

`pycounts` was created by Tomas Beuzen. It is licensed under the terms
of the MIT license.

Credits

`pycounts` was created with
[`cookiecutter`](https://cookiecutter.readthedocs.io/en/latest/) and
the `py-pkgs-cookiecutter`
[template](https://github.com/py-pkgs/py-pkgs-cookiecutter).

When we render this Markdown text later on with sphinx, it will look like Fig. 3.5. We'll talk about sphinx in **Section 3.8.4**, but many other tools are also able to natively render Markdown documents (e.g., Jupyter, VS Code, GitHub, etc.), which is why it's so widely used.

FIGURE 3.5: Rendered version of README.md.

So, we now have a *CHANGELOG.md*, *CONDUCT.md*, *CONTRIBUTING.md*, *LICENSE*, and *README.md*. In the next section, we'll explain how to document your package's Python code using docstrings.

3.8.2 Writing docstrings

A docstring is a string, surrounded by triple-quotes, at the start of a module, class, or function in Python (preceding any code) that provides documentation on what the object does and how to use it. Docstrings automatically become the documented object's documentation, accessible to users via the help() function. Docstrings are a user's first port-of-call when they are trying to use your package, they really are a necessity when creating packages, even for yourself.

General docstring convention in Python is described in Python Enhancement Proposal (PEP) 257 — Docstring Conventions[24], but there is flexibility in how you write your docstrings. A minimal docstring contains a single line describing what the object does, and that might be sufficient for a simple function or for when your code is in the early stages of development. However, for code you intend to share with others (including your future self) a more comprehensive docstring should be written. A typical docstring will include:

1. A one-line summary that does not use variable names or the function name.
2. An extended description.
3. Parameter types and descriptions.
4. Returned value types and descriptions.
5. Example usage.
6. Potentially more.

There are different "docstring styles" used in Python to organize this information, such as numpydoc style[25], Google style[26], and sphinx style[27]. We'll be using the numpydoc style for our pycounts package because it is readable, commonly used, and supported by sphinx. In the numpydoc style:

- Section headers are denoted as text underlined with dashes;

```
Parameters
----------
```

- Input arguments are denoted as:

```
name : type
    Description of parameter `name`.
```

- Output values use the same syntax above, but specifying the name is optional.

We show a numpydoc style docstring for our count_words() function below:

---

[24]https://www.python.org/dev/peps/pep-0257/

[25]https://numpydoc.readthedocs.io/en/latest/format.html#docstring-standard

[26]https://github.com/google/styleguide/blob/gh-pages/pyguide.md#38-comments-and-docstrings

[27]https://sphinx-rtd-tutorial.readthedocs.io/en/latest/docstrings.html#the-sphinx-docstring-format

```python
def count_words(input_file):
    """Count words in a text file.

    Words are made lowercase and punctuation is removed
    before counting.

    Parameters
    ----------
    input_file : str
        Path to text file.

    Returns
    -------
    collections.Counter
        dict-like object where keys are words and values are counts.

    Examples
    --------
    >>> count_words("text.txt")
    """
    text = load_text(input_file)
    text = clean_text(text)
    words = text.split()
    return Counter(words)
```

This docstrings can be accessed by users of our package by using the `help()` function in a Python interpreter:

```python
>>> from pycounts.pycounts import count_words
>>> help(count_words)
```

```
Help on function count_words in module pycounts.pycounts:

count_words(input_file)
    Count words in a text file.

    Words are made lowercase and punctuation is removed
    before counting.

    Parameters
    ----------
    ...
```

You can add information to your docstrings at your discretion — you won't always need all the sections above, and in some cases you may want to include additional sections from the numpydoc style documentation[28]. We've documented the remaining functions from our `pycounts` package as below. If you're following along with this tutorial, copy these docstrings into the functions in the `pycounts.pycounts` and `pycounts.plotting` modules:

```python
def plot_words(word_counts, n=10):
    """Plot a bar chart of word counts.

    Parameters
    ----------
    word_counts : collections.Counter
        Counter object of word counts.
    n : int, optional
        Plot the top n words. By default, 10.

    Returns
    -------
    matplotlib.container.BarContainer
        Bar chart of word counts.

    Examples
    --------
    >>> from pycounts.pycounts import count_words
    >>> from pycounts.plotting import plot_words
    >>> counts = count_words("text.txt")
    >>> plot_words(counts)
    """
    top_n_words = word_counts.most_common(n)
    word, count = zip(*top_n_words)
    fig = plt.bar(range(n), count)
    plt.xticks(range(n), labels=word, rotation=45)
    plt.xlabel("Word")
    plt.ylabel("Count")
    return fig
```

---

[28] https://numpydoc.readthedocs.io/en/latest/format.html#docstring-standard

```python
def load_text(input_file):
    """Load text from a text file and return as a string.

    Parameters
    ----------
    input_file : str
        Path to text file.

    Returns
    -------
    str
        Text file contents.

    Examples
    --------
    >>> load_text("text.txt")
    """
    with open(input_file, "r") as file:
        text = file.read()
    return text


def clean_text(text):
    """Lowercase and remove punctuation from a string.

    Parameters
    ----------
    text : str
        Text to clean.

    Returns
    -------
    str
        Cleaned text.

    Examples
    --------
    >>> clean_text("Early optimization is the root of all evil!")
    'early optimization is the root of all evil'
    """
    text = text.lower()
    for p in punctuation:
        text = text.replace(p, "")
    return text
```

For the users of our package it would be helpful to compile all of our functions and docstrings into a easy-to-navigate document, so they can access this documentation without having to `import` them and run `help()`, or search through our source code. Such a document is referred to as an application programming interface (API) reference. We could create one by manually copying and pasting all of our function names and docstrings into a plain-text file, but that would be inefficient. Instead, we'll show how to use `sphinx` in **Section 3.8.4** to automatically parse our source code, extract our functions and docstrings, and create an API reference for us.

3.8.3 Creating usage examples

Creating examples of how to use your package can be invaluable to new and existing users alike. Unlike the brief and basic "Usage" heading we wrote in our README in **Section 3.8.1**, these examples are more like tutorials, including a mix of text and code that demonstrates the functionality and common workflows of your package step-by-step.

You could write examples from scratch using a plain-text format like Markdown, but this can be inefficient and prone to errors. If you change the way a function works, or what it outputs, you would have to re-write your example. Instead, in this section we'll show how to use Jupyter Notebooks (Kluyver et al., 2016) as a more efficient, interactive, and reproducible way to create usage examples for your users. If you don't want to create usage examples for your package, or aren't interested in learning how to use Jupyter Notebooks to do so, you can skip to **Section 3.8.4**.

Jupyter Notebooks are interactive documents with an *.ipynb* extension that can contain code, equations, text, and visualizations. They are effective for demonstrating examples because they directly import and use code from your package; this ensures you don't make mistakes when writing out your examples, and it allows users to download, execute, and interact with the notebooks themselves (as opposed to just reading text). To create a usage example for our `pycounts` package using a Jupyter Notebook, we first need to add `jupyter` as a development dependency:

If using a `conda` virtual environment, make sure that environment is active by running `conda activate pycounts`, before using or working on your package.

```
$ poetry add --dev jupyter
```

Our `py-pkgs-cookiecutter` template already created a Jupyter Notebook example document for us at *docs/example.ipynb*. To edit that document, we first open the Jupyter Notebook application using the following command from the root package directory:

```
$ jupyter notebook
```

If you're developing your Python package in an IDE that natively supports Jupyter Notebooks, such as Visual Studio Code or JupyterLab, you can simply open *docs/example.ipynb* to edit it, without needing to run the `jupyter notebook` command above.

In the interface, navigate to and open *docs/example.ipynb*. As explained in the Jupyter Notebook documentation[29], notebooks are comprised of "cells", which can contain Python code or Markdown text. Our notebook currently looks like Fig. 3.6.

As an example, we'll update our notebook with the collection of Markdown and code cells shown in Fig. 3.7 and Fig. 3.8.

Our Jupyter Notebook now contains an interactive tutorial demonstrating the basic usage of our package. What's important to note is that the code and outputs are generated using our package itself, they have not been written manually. Our users could now also download our example notebook and interact and execute it themselves. But in the next section, we'll show how to use `sphinx` to automatically execute notebooks and include their content (including the outputs of code cells) into a compiled collection of all our package's documentation that users can easily read and navigate through without even having to start the Jupyter application!

3.8.4 Building documentation

We've now written all the individual pieces of documentation needed to support our `pycounts` package. But all this documentation is spread over the

---
[29]https://jupyter-notebook.readthedocs.io/en/stable/

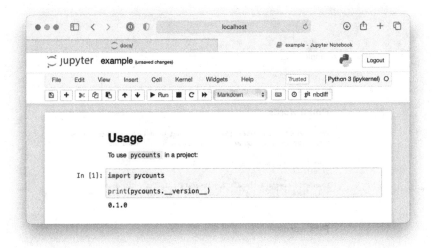

FIGURE 3.6: A simple Jupyter Notebook using code from pycounts.

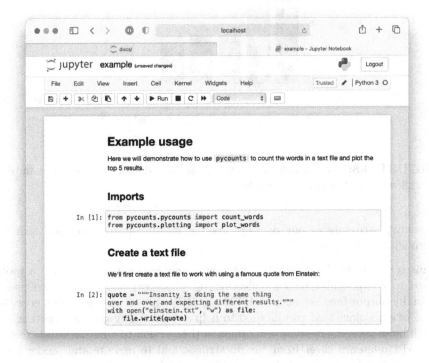

FIGURE 3.7: First half of Jupyter Notebook demonstrating an example workflow using the pycounts package.

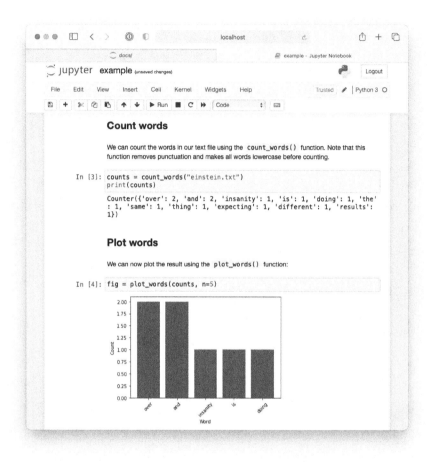

FIGURE 3.8: Second half of Jupyter Notebook demonstrating an example workflow using the pycounts package.

directory structure of our package making it difficult to share and search through.

This is where the documentation generator sphinx comes in. sphinx is a tool used to compile and render collections of plain-text source files into user-friendly output formats, such as HTML or PDF. sphinx also has a rich ecosystem of extensions that can be used to help automatically generate content — we'll be using some of these extensions in this section to automatically create an API reference sheet from our docstrings, and to execute and render our Jupyter Notebook example into our documentation.

To first give you an idea of what we're going to build, Fig. 3.9 shows the homepage of our package's documentation compiled by sphinx into HTML.

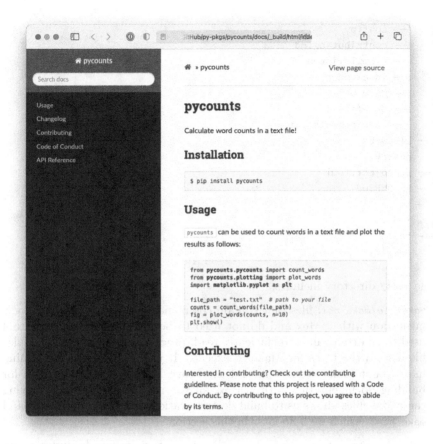

FIGURE 3.9: The documentation homepage generated by sphinx.

The source and configuration files to build documentation like this using sphinx typically live in the *docs/* directory in a package's root. The py-pkgs-cookiecutter automatically created this directory and the necessary files for us. We'll discuss what each of these files are used for below.

```
pycounts
├── .readthedocs.yml
├── CHANGELOG.md
├── CONDUCT.md
├── CONTRIBUTING.md
├── docs
│   ├── changelog.md
│   ├── conduct.md
```

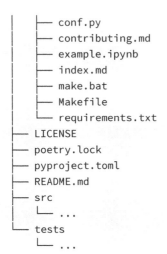

```
|     ├── conf.py
|     ├── contributing.md
|     ├── example.ipynb
|     ├── index.md
|     ├── make.bat
|     ├── Makefile
|     └── requirements.txt
├── LICENSE
├── poetry.lock
├── pyproject.toml
├── README.md
├── src
|   └── ...
└── tests
    └── ...
```

The *docs/* directory includes:

- *Makefile/make.bat*: files that contain commands needed to build our documentation with sphinx and do not need to be modified. Make[30] is a tool used to run commands to efficiently read, process, and write files. A Makefile defines the tasks for Make to execute. If you're interested in learning more about Make, we recommend the Learn Makefiles[31] tutorial. But for building documentation with sphinx, all you need to know is that having these Makefiles allows us to build documentation with the simple command make html, which we'll do later in this section.

- *requirements.txt*: contains a list of documentation-specific dependencies required to host our documentation online on Read the Docs[32], which we'll discuss in **Section 3.8.5**.

- *conf.py* is a configuration file controlling how sphinx builds your documentation. You can read more about *conf.py* in the sphinx documentation[33] and we'll touch on it again shortly, but, for now, it has been pre-populated by the py-pkgs-cookiecutter template and does not need to be modified.

- The remaining files in the *docs/* directory form the content of our generated documentation, as we'll discuss in the remainder of this section.

The *index.md* file will form the landing page of our documentation (the one we saw earlier in Fig. 3.9). Think of it as the homepage of a website. For your landing page, you'd typically want some high-level information about your package, and then links to the rest of the documentation you want to expose

---

[30]https://www.gnu.org/software/make/
[31]https://makefiletutorial.com
[32]https://readthedocs.org/
[33]https://www.sphinx-doc.org/en/master/usage/configuration.html

to a user. If you open *index.md* in an editor of your choice, that's exactly the content we are including, with a particular kind of syntax, which we explain below.

```
```{include} ../README.md
```
```

```
```toctree
:maxdepth: 1
:hidden:

example.ipynb
changelog.md
contributing.md
conduct.md
autoapi/index
```
```

The syntax we're using in this file is known as Markedly Structured Text (MyST)[34]. MyST is based on Markdown but with additional syntax options compatible for use with sphinx. The {include} syntax specifies that when this page is rendered with sphinx, we want it to include the content of the *README.md* from our package's root directory (think of it as a copy-paste operation).

The {toctree} syntax defines what documents will be listed in the table of contents (ToC) on the left-hand side of our rendered documentation, as shown in Fig. 3.9. The argument :maxdepth: 1 indicates how many heading levels the ToC should include, and :hidden: specifies that the ToC should only appear in the side bar and not in the welcome page itself. The ToC then lists the documents to include in our rendered documentation.

"example.ipynb" is the Jupyter Notebook we wrote in section **Section 3.8.3**. sphinx doesn't support relative links in a ToC, so to include the documents *CHANGELOG.md*, *CONTRIBUTING.md*, *CONDUCT.md* from our package's root, we create "stub files" called *changelog.md*, *contributing.md*, and *conduct.md*, which link to these documents using the {include} syntax we saw earlier. For example, *changelog.md* contains the following text:

```
```{include} ../CHANGELOG.md
```
```

The final document in the ToC, "autoapi/index" is an API reference sheet

---

[34]https://myst-parser.readthedocs.io/en/latest/syntax/syntax.html

that will be generated automatically for us, from our package structure and docstrings, when we build our documentation with `sphinx`.

Before we can go ahead and build our documentation with `sphinx`, it relies on a few `sphinx` extensions that need to be installed and configured:

- myst-nb[35]: extension that will enable `sphinx` to parse our Markdown, MyST, and Jupyter Notebook files (`sphinx` only supports reStructuredTex, *.rst* files, by default).
- sphinx-rtd-theme[36]: a custom theme for styling the way our documentation will look. It looks much better than the default theme.
- sphinx-autoapi[37]: extension that will parse our source code and docstrings to create an API reference sheet.
- sphinx.ext.napoleon[38]: extension that enables `sphinx` to parse numpydoc style docstrings.
- sphinx.ext.viewcode[39]: extension that adds a helpful link to the source code of each object in the API reference sheet.

These extensions are not necessary to create documentation with `sphinx`, but they are all commonly used in Python packaging documentation and significantly improve the look and user-experience of the generated documentation. Extensions without the `sphinx.ext` prefix need to be installed. We can install them as development dependencies in a `poetry`-managed project with the following command:

If using a `conda` virtual environment, make sure that environment is active by running `conda activate pycounts`, before using or working on your package.

```
$ poetry add --dev myst-nb --python "^3.9"
$ poetry add --dev sphinx-autoapi sphinx-rtd-theme
```

Adding `myst-nb` is a great example of why upper caps on dependency versions can be a pain, as we discussed in **Section**

---

[35]https://myst-nb.readthedocs.io/en/latest/

[36]https://sphinx-rtd-theme.readthedocs.io/en/stable/

[37]https://sphinx-autoapi.readthedocs.io/en/latest/

[38]https://sphinxcontrib-napoleon.readthedocs.io/en/latest/

[39]https://www.sphinx-doc.org/en/master/usage/extensions/viewcode.html

3.6.1. At the time of writing, one of the dependencies of myst-nb, mdit-py-plugins, has an upper cap of <4.0 on the Python version it requires, so it's not compatible with our package and its other dependencies which all support Python >=3.9. Thus, unless mdit-py-plugins removes this upper cap, the easiest way for us to add myst-nb is to tell poetry to only install it for Python versions ^3.9 (i.e., >=3.9 and <4.0), by using the argument --python "^3.9".

Once installed, any extensions you want to use need to be added to a list called extensions in the *conf.py* configuration file and configured. Configuration options for each extension (if they exist) can be viewed in their respective documentation, but the py-pkgs-cookiecutter has already taken care of everything for us, by defining the following variables within *conf.py*:

```
extensions = [
    "myst_nb",
    "autoapi.extension",
    "sphinx.ext.napoleon",
    "sphinx.ext.viewcode"
]
autoapi_dirs = ["../src"]  # location to parse for API reference
html_theme = "sphinx_rtd_theme"
```

With our documentation structure set up, and our extensions configured, we can now navigate to the *docs/* directory and build our documentation with sphinx using the following commands:

```
$ cd docs
$ make html
```

```
Running Sphinx
...
build succeeded.
The HTML pages are in _build/html.
```

If we look inside our *docs/* directory we see a new directory *_build/html*, which contains our built documentation as HTML files. If you open *_build/html/index.html*, you should see the page shown earlier in Fig. 3.9.

If you make significant changes to your documentation, it can be a good idea to delete the `_build/` folder before building it again. You can do this easily by adding the `clean` option into the `make html` command: `make clean html`.

The `sphinx-autoapi` extension extracted the docstrings we wrote for our package's functions in **Fig. @ref(fig:03:Writing-docstrings** and rendered them into our documentation. You can find the generated API reference sheet by clicking "API Reference" in the table of contents. For example, {numref}03-documentation-2-fig) shows the functions and docstrings in the `pycounts.plotting` module. The `sphinx.ext.viewcode` extension added the "source" button next to each function in our API reference sheet, which links readers directly to the source code of the function (if they want to view it).

Finally, if we navigate to the "Example usage" page, Fig. 3.11 shows the Jupyter Notebook we wrote in **Section 3.8.3** rendered into our documentation, including the Markdown text, code input, and executed output. This was made possible using the `myst-nb` extension.

Ultimately, you can efficiently make beautiful and many-featured documentation with `sphinx` and its ecosystem of extensions. You can now use this documentation yourself or potentially share it with others, but it really shines when you host it on the web using a free service like Read the Docs[40], as we'll do in the next section. For those using version control, now is a good time to move back to our package's root directory and commit our work using the following commands:

```
$ cd ..
$ git add README.md docs/example.ipynb
$ git commit -m "docs: updated readme and example"
$ git add src/pycounts/pycounts.py src/pycounts/plotting.py
$ git commit -m "docs: created docstrings for package functions"
$ git add pyproject.toml poetry.lock
$ git commit -m "build: added dev dependencies for docs"
$ git push
```

---

[40]https://readthedocs.org/

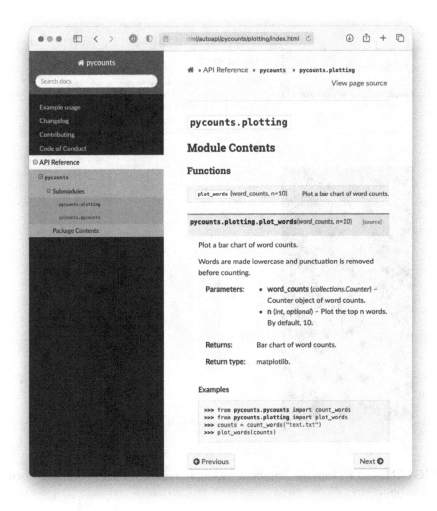

FIGURE 3.10: Documentation for the pycounts plotting module.

3.8.5 Hosting documentation online

If you intend to share your package with others, it will be useful to make your documentation accessible online. It's common to host Python package documentation on the free online hosting service Read the Docs[41]. Read the Docs works by connecting to an online repository hosting your package documentation, such as a GitHub repository. When you push changes to your repository, Read the Docs automatically builds a fresh copy of your documentation (i.e., runs make html) and hosts it at the URL https://<pkgname>.readthedocs.io/

---

[41]https://readthedocs.org/

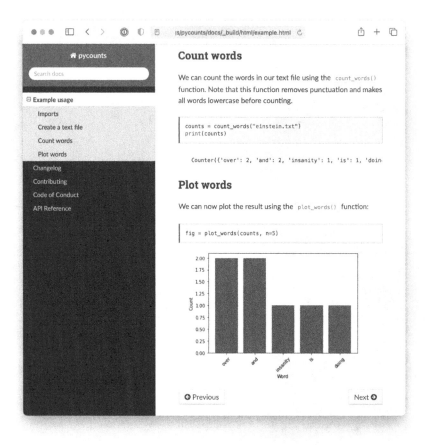

FIGURE 3.11: Jupyter Notebook example rendered into pycounts's documentation.

(you can also configure Read the Docs to use a custom domain name). This means that any changes you make to your documentation source files (and push to your linked remote repository) are immediately deployed to your users. If you need your documentation to be private (e.g., only available to employees of a company), Read the Docs offers a paid "Business plan" with this functionality.

GitHub Pages[42] is another popular service used for hosting documentation from a repository. However, it doesn't natively support automatic building of your documentation when you push changes to the source files, which is why we prefer to use Read the Docs here. If you did want to host your docs on GitHub Pages, we recommend using the ghp-import[43] package, or setting up an automated GitHub Actions workflow using the peaceiris/actions-gh-pages[44] action (we'll learn more about GitHub Actions in **Chapter 8: Continuous integration and deployment**).

The Read the Docs[45] documentation will provide the most up-to-date steps required to host your documentation online. For our `pycounts` package, this involved the following steps:

1. Visit `https://readthedocs.org/` and click on "Sign up".
2. Select "Sign up with GitHub".
3. Click "Import a Project".
4. Click "Import Manually".
5. Fill in the project details by:
   1. Providing your package name (e.g., `pycounts`).
   2. The URL to your package's GitHub repository (e.g., `https://github.com/TomasBeuzen/pycounts`).
   3. Specify the default branch as `main`.
6. Click "Next" and then "Build version".

After following the steps above, your documentation should be successfully built by Read the Docs[46], and you should be able to access it via the "View Docs" button on the build page. For example, the documentation for `pycounts` is now available at `https://pycounts.readthedocs.io/en/latest/`. This documentation will be automatically re-built by Read the Docs each time you push changes to your GitHub repository.

---

[42]`https://pages.github.com`
[43]`https://github.com/c-w/ghp-import`
[44]`https://github.com/peaceiris/actions-gh-pages`
[45]`https://readthedocs.org`
[46]`https://readthedocs.org/`

The *.readthedocs.yml* file that `py-pkgs-cookiecutter` created
for us in the root directory of our Python package contains the
configuration settings necessary for Read the Docs to properly
build our documentation. It specifies what version of Python to
use and tells Read the Docs that our documentation requires the
extra packages specified in *pycounts/docs/requirements.txt* to
be generated correctly.

3.9   Tagging a package release with version control

We have now created all the source files that make up version 0.1.0 of our
`pycounts` package, including Python code, documentation, and tests — well
done! In the next section, we'll turn all these source files into a distribution
package that can be easily shared and installed by others. But for those using
version control, it's helpful at this point to tag a release of your package's
repository. If you're not using version control, you can skip to **Section 3.10**.

Tagging a release means that we permanently "tag" a specific point in our
repository's history, and then create a downloadable "release" of all the files
in our repository in the state they were in when the tag was made. It's common
to tag a release for each new version of your package, as we'll discuss more in
Chapter 7: Releasing and versioning.

Tagging a release is a two-step process involving both Git and GitHub:

1. Create a tag marking a specific point in a repository's history using
   the command `git tag`.
2. On GitHub, create a release of all the files in your repository (usually
   in the form of a zipped archive like *.zip* or *.tar.gz*) based on your
   tag. Others can then download this release if they wish to view or
   use your package's source files as they existed at the time the tag
   was created.

We'll demonstrate this process by tagging a release of v0.1.0 of our `pycounts`
package (it's common to prefix a tag with "v" for "version"). First, we need
to create a tag identifying the state of our repository at v0.1.0 and then push
the tag to GitHub using the following `git` commands at the command line:

```
$ git tag v0.1.0
$ git push --tags
```

Now if you go to the `pycounts` repository on GitHub and navigate to the "Releases" tab, you should see a tag like that shown in Fig. 3.12.

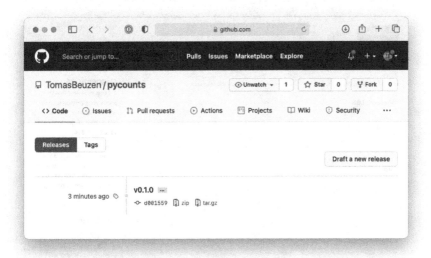

FIGURE 3.12: Tag of v0.1.0 of pycounts on GitHub.

To create a release from this tag, click "Draft a new release". You can then identify the tag from which to create the release and optionally add some additional details about the release as shown in Fig. 3.13.

After clicking "Publish release", GitHub will automatically create a release from your tag, including compressed archives of your code in *.zip* and *.tar.gz* format, as shown in Fig. 3.14.

We'll talk more about making new versions and releases of your package as you update it (e.g., modify code, add features, fix bugs, etc.) in **Chapter 7: Releasing and versioning**.

People with access to your GitHub repository can actually `pip install` your package directly from the repository using your tags. We talk more about that in **Section 4.3.4**.

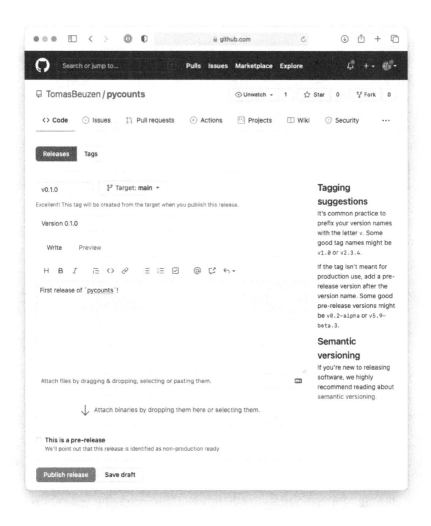

FIGURE 3.13: Making a release of v0.1.0 of pycounts on GitHub.

3.10 Building and distributing your package

3.10.1 Building your package

Right now, our package is a collection of files and folders that is difficult to share with others. The solution to this problem is to create a "distribution package". A distribution package is a single archive file containing all

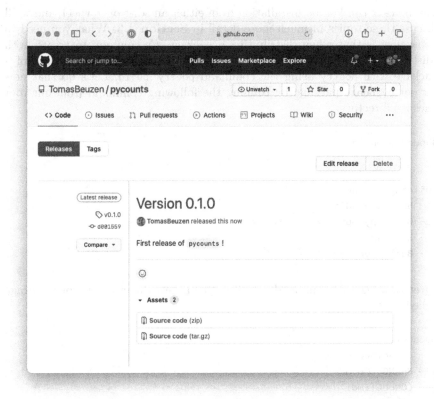

FIGURE 3.14: Release of v0.1.0 of pycounts on GitHub.

the files and information necessary to install a package using a tool like pip. Distribution packages are often called "distributions" for short and they are how packages are shared in Python and installed by users, typically with the command pip install <some-package>.

The main types of distributions in Python are source distributions (known as "sdists") and wheels. sdists are a compressed archive of all the source files, metadata, and instructions needed to construct an installable version of your package. To install from an sdist, a user needs to download the sdist, extract its contents, and then use the build instructions to build and finally install the package on their computer.

In contrast, wheels are pre-built versions of a package. They are built on the developer's machine before sharing with users. They are the preferred distribution format because a user only needs to download the wheel and move it to the location on their computer where Python searches for packages; no build step is required.

`pip install` can handle installation from either an sdist or a wheel, and we'll discuss these topics in much more detail in **Section 4.3**. What you need to know now is that when distributing a package it's common to create both sdist and wheel distributions. We can easily create an sdist and wheel of a package with `poetry` using the command `poetry build`. Let's do that now for our `pycounts` package by running the following command from our root package directory:

```
$ poetry build
```

```
Building pycounts (0.1.0)
  - Building sdist
  - Built pycounts-0.1.0.tar.gz
  - Building wheel
  - Built pycounts-0.1.0-py3-none-any.whl
```

After running this command, you'll notice a new directory in your package called *dist/*:

```
pycounts
├── .readthedocs.yml
├── CHANGELOG.md
├── CONDUCT.md
├── CONTRIBUTING.md
├── dist
│   ├── pycounts-0.1.0-py3-none-any.whl   <- wheel
│   └── pycounts-0.1.0.tar.gz             <- sdist
├── docs
│   └── ...
├── LICENSE
├── poetry.lock
├── pyproject.toml
├── README.md
├── src
│   └── ...
└── tests
    └── ...
```

Those two new files are the sdist and wheel for our `pycounts` package. A user could now easily install our package if they had one of these distributions by using `pip install`. For example, to install the wheel (the preferred distribution type), you could enter the following in a terminal:

```
$ cd dist/
$ pip install pycounts-0.1.0-py3-none-any.whl
```

```
Processing ./pycounts-0.1.0-py3-none-any.whl
...
Successfully installed pycounts-0.1.0
```

To install using the sdist, you would have to unpack the sdist archive before running `pip install`. The procedure for this varies depending on your specific operating system. For example, on Mac OS, the command line tool `tar` with argument `x` (extract the input file), `z` (gunzip the input file), `f` (apply operations to the provided input file) can be used to unpack the sdist:

```
$ tar xzf pycounts-0.1.0.tar.gz
$ pip install pycounts-0.1.0/
```

```
Processing ./pycounts-0.1.0-py3-none-any.whl
  Installing build dependencies ... done
    Getting requirements to build wheel ... done
    Preparing wheel metadata ... done
...
Successfully built pycounts
Successfully installed pycounts-0.1.0
```

Note in the output above how installing from an sdist requires a build step prior to installation. The sdist is first built into a wheel, which is then installed. For those interested, we discuss the nuances of building and installing packages from sdists and wheels in **Section 4.3**.

Creating a distribution for our package is most useful if we make it available on an online repository like the Python Package Index (PyPI), the official online software repository for Python. This would allow users to simply run `pip install pycounts` to install our package, without needing the sdist or wheel files locally, and we'll do this in the next section. But even if you don't intend to share your package, it can still be useful to build and install distributions for two reasons:

1. A distribution is a self-contained copy of your package's source files that's easy to move around and store on your computer. It makes it easy to retain distributions for different versions of your package, so that you can re-use or share them if you ever need to.
2. Recall that `poetry` installs package in "editable mode", such that a

link to the package's location is installed, rather than an independent distribution of the package itself. This is useful for *development purposes*, because it means that any changes to the source code will be immediately reflected when you next import the package, without the need to poetry install again. However, for *users* of your package (including yourself using your package in other projects), it is often better to install a "non-editable" version of the package (the default behavior when you pip install an sdist or wheel) because a non-editable installation will remain stable and immune to any changes made to the source files on your computer.

3.10.2   Publishing to TestPyPI

At this point, we have distributions of pycounts that we want to share with the world by publishing to PyPI[47]. However, it is good practice to do a "dry run" and check that everything works as expected by submitting to TestPyPi[48] first. poetry has a publish command, which we can use to do this, however the default behavior is to publish to PyPI. So we need to add TestPyPI to the list of repositories poetry knows about using the following command:

```
$ poetry config repositories.test-pypi https://test.pypi.org/legacy/
```

To publish to TestPyPI we can use poetry publish (you will be prompted for your username and password for TestPyPI — which we signed up for in **Section 2.3**):

```
$ poetry publish -r test-pypi
```

```
Username: TomasBeuzen
Password:
Publishing pycounts (0.1.0) to test-pypi
  - Uploading pycounts-0.1.0-py3-none-any.whl 100%
  - Uploading pycounts-0.1.0.tar.gz 100%
```

Rather than entering your username and password every time you want to publish a distribution to TestPyPI or PyPI, you

---

[47]https://pypi.org/
[48]https://test.pypi.org/

can configure an API token as described in the PyPI documentation[49].

Now we should be able to visit our package on TestPyPI. The URL for our `pycounts` package is: `https://test.pypi.org/project/pycounts/`. We can try installing our package using `pip` from the command line with the following command:

```
$ pip install --index-url https://test.pypi.org/simple/ \
  --extra-index-url https://pypi.org/simple \
  pycounts
```

By default `pip install` will search PyPI for the named package. However, we want to search TestPyPI because that is where we uploaded our package. The argument `--index-url` points `pip` to the TestPyPI index. However, it's important to note that not all developers upload their packages to TestPyPI; some only upload them directly to PyPI. If your package depends on packages that are not on TestPyPI you can tell `pip` to try and look for them on PyPI instead. To do that, you can use the argument `--extra-index-url` as we do in the command above.

3.10.3 Publishing to PyPI

If you were able to upload your package to TestPyPI and install it without error, you're ready to publish your package to PyPI. You can publish to PyPI using the `poetry publish` command without any arguments:

```
$ poetry publish
```

Your package will then be available on PyPI (e.g., `https://pypi.org/project/pycounts/`) and can be installed by anyone using `pip`:

```
$ pip install pycounts
```

3.11 Summary and next steps

This chapter provided a practical overview of the key steps required to generate a fully-featured Python package. In the following chapters, we'll explore

---

[49]`https://pypi.org/help/#apitoken`

each of these steps in more detail and continue to add features to our `pycounts` package. Two key workflows we have yet to discuss are:

1. Releasing new versions of your package as you update it. We'll discuss this in **Chapter 7: Releasing and versioning**.
2. Setting up continuous integration and continuous deployment (CI/CD) — that is, automated pipelines for running tests, building documentation, and deploying your package. We'll discuss CI/CD in **Chapter 8: Continuous integration and deployment**.

Before moving onto the next chapter, let's summarize a reference list of all the steps we took to develop a Python package in this chapter:

1. Create package structure using `cookiecutter` (**Section 3.2.2**).

   ```
   $ cookiecutter \
     https://github.com/py-pkgs/py-pkgs-cookiecutter.git
   ```

2. (Optional) Put your package under version control (**Section 3.3**).

3. (Optional) Create and activate a virtual environment using `conda` (**Section 3.5.1**).

   ```
   $ conda create --name <your-env-name> python=3.9 -y
   $ conda activate <your-env-name>
   ```

4. Add Python code to module(s) in the `src/` directory (**Section 3.4**), adding dependencies as needed (**Section 3.6**).

   ```
   $ poetry add <dependency>
   ```

5. Install and try out your package in a Python interpreter (**Section 3.5.2**).

   ```
   $ poetry install
   ```

6. (Optional) Write tests for your package in module(s) prefixed with `test_` in the `tests/` directory. Add `pytest` as a development dependency to run your tests (**Section 3.7.2**). Add `pytest-cov` as

a development dependency to calculate the coverage of your tests (**Section 3.7.3**).

```
$ poetry add --dev pytest pytest-cov
$ pytest tests/ --cov=<pkg-name>
```

7. (Optional) Create documentation source files for your package (**Section 3.8**). Use sphinx to compile and generate an HTML render of your documentation, adding the required development dependencies (**Section 3.8.4**).

```
$ poetry add --dev myst-nb sphinx-autoapi sphinx-rtd-theme
$ cd docs
$ make html
$ cd ..
```

8. (Optional) Host documentation online with Read the Docs[50] (**Section 3.8.5**).

9. (Optional) Tag a release of your package using Git and GitHub, or equivalent version control tools (**Section 3.9**).

10. Build sdist and wheel distributions for your package (**Section 3.10.1**).

```
$ poetry build
```

11. (Optional) Publish your distributions to TestPyPI[51] and try installing your package (**Section 3.10.2**).

```
$ poetry config repositories.test-pypi \
  https://test.pypi.org/legacy/
$ poetry publish -r test-pypi
$ pip install --index-url https://test.pypi.org/simple/ \
  --extra-index-url https://pypi.org/simple \
  pycounts
```

---

[50]https://readthedocs.org/
[51]https://test.pypi.org/

12. (Optional) Publish your distributions to PyPI[52]. Your package can now be installed by anyone using `pip` (**Section 3.10.3**).

```
$ poetry publish
$ pip install <pkg-name>
```

The above workflow uses a particular suite of tools (e.g., `conda`, `poetry`, `sphinx`, etc.) to develop a Python package. While there are other tools that can be used to help build Python packages, the aim of this book is to give a high-level, practical, and efficient introduction to Python packaging using modern tools, and this has influenced our selection of tools in this chapter and book. However, the concepts and workflow discussed here remain relevant to the Python packaging ecosystem, regardless of the exact tools you use to develop your Python packages.

---

[52]`https://pypi.org/`

4

Package structure and distribution

Chapter 3: How to package a Python provided a practical overview of how to create, install, and distribute a Python package. This chapter now goes into more detail about what a Python package actually is, digging deeper into how packages are structured, installed, and distributed.

We begin with a discussion of how modules and packages are represented in Python and why they are used. We then discuss some more advanced package structure topics, such as controlling the import behavior of a package and including non-code files, like data. The chapter finishes with a discussion of what package distributions are, how to build them, and how they are installed. Along the way, we'll demonstrate key concepts by continuing to develop our pycounts package from the previous chapter.

4.1 Packaging fundamentals

We'll begin this chapter by exploring some of the lower-level implementation details related to what packages are, how they're structured, and how they're used in Python.

All data in a Python program are represented by objects or by relations between objects. For example, integers and functions are kinds of Python objects. We can find the type of a Python object using the `type()` function. For example, the code below, run in a Python interpreter, creates an integer object and a function object mapped to the names a and `hello_world`, respectively:

```
>>> a = 1
>>> type(a)
```

```
int
```

```
>>> def hello_world(name):
        print(f"Hello world! My name is {name}.")
>>> type(hello_world)
```

```
function
```

The Python object important to our discussion of packages is the "module" object. A module is an object that serves as an organizational unit of Python code. Typically, Python code you want to reuse is stored in a file with a *.py* suffix and is imported using the `import` statement. This process creates a module object with the same name as the imported file (excluding the *.py* suffix), and from this object, we can access the contents of the file.

For example, imagine we have a module *greetings.py* in our current directory containing functions to print "Hello World!" in English and Squamish (the Squamish people[1] are an indigenous people of modern-day British Columbia, Canada):

```
def hello_world():
    print("Hello World!")

def hello_world_squamish():
    print("I chen tl'ik̲!")
```

We can import that module using the `import` statement and can use the `type()` function to verify that we created a module object, which has been mapped to the name "greetings" (the name of the file):

```
>>> import greetings
>>> type(greetings)
```

```
module
```

We call the module object an "organizational unit of code" because the content of the module (in this case, the two "hello world" functions) can be accessed via the module name and "dot notation". For example:

---

[1] https://en.wikipedia.org/wiki/Squamish_people

```
>>> greetings.hello_world()
```

```
"Hello World!"
```

```
>>> greetings.hello_world_squamish()
```

```
"I chen tl'iḵ!"
```

At this point in our discussion, it's useful to mention Python's namespaces. A "namespace" in Python is a mapping from names to objects. From the code examples above, we've added the names a (an integer), hello_world (a function), and greetings (a module) to the current namespace and can use those names to refer to the objects we created. The dir() function can be used to inspect a namespace. When called with no arguments, dir() returns a list of names defined in the current namespace:

```
>>> dir()
```

```
['__annotations__', '__builtins__', '__doc__', '__loader__',
 '__name__', '__package__', '__spec__', 'a', 'hello_world',
 'greetings']
```

In the output above, we can see the names of the three objects we have defined in this section: a, hello_world, and greetings. The other names bounded by double underscores are objects that were initialized automatically when we started the Python interpreter and are implementation details that aren't important to our discussion here but can be read about in the Python documentation[2].

Namespaces are created at different moments, have different lifetimes, and can be accessed from different parts of a Python program — but these details digress from our discussion, and we point interested readers to the Python documentation[3] to learn more. The important point to make here is that when a module is imported using the import statement, a module object is created and it has its own namespace containing the names of the Python objects defined in the modules. For example, when we imported the *greetings.py* file earlier, we created a greetings module object and namespace containing the names

---

[2]https://docs.python.org/3/reference/executionmodel.html?highlight=__builtins__#exe
cution-model

[3]https://docs.python.org/3/tutorial/classes.html#python-scopes-and-namespaces

of the objects defined in the file — `hello_world` and `hello_world_squamish` —
which we can access using dot notation, e.g., `greetings.hello_world()` and
`greetings.hello_world_squamish()`.

In this way, the module object isolates a collection of code and provides us with
a clean, logical, and organized way to access it. We can inspect the namespace
of a module by passing the module object as an input to the `dir()` function:

```
>>> dir(greetings)
```

```
['__annotations__', '__builtins__', '__doc__', '__loader__',
 '__name__', '__package__', '__spec__', 'hello_world',
 'hello_world_squamish']
```

An important point to stress here is that there is no relation between names in
different namespaces. That means that we can have objects of the exact same
name in a Python session if they exist in different namespaces. For example,
in the Python session we've been running in this section we have access to
two `hello_world` functions; one that was defined earlier in our interactive
interpreter, and one defined in the `greetings` module. While these functions
have the exact same name, there is no relation between them because they
exist in different namespaces; `greetings.hello_world()` exists in the `greetings`
module namespace, and `hello_world()` exists in the "global" namespace of our
interpreter. So, we can access both with the appropriate syntax:

```
>>> hello_world("Tom")
```

```
"Hello world! My name is Tom."
```

```
>>> greetings.hello_world()
```

```
"Hello World!"
```

Now that we have a basic understanding of modules, we can further discuss
packages. Packages are just a collection of one or more modules. They are typically structured as a directory (the package) containing one or more *.py* files
(the modules) and/or subdirectories (which we call subpackages). A special file
named *__init__.py* is used to tell Python that a directory is a package (rather
than just a plain-old directory on your computer). We'll talk more about the
__init__.py file and package structure in **Section 3.2**, but for now, here's an
example of a simple package structure with two modules and one subpackage:

```
pkg
├── __init__.py
├── module1.py
└── subpkg
    ├── __init__.py
    └── module2.py
```

Put simply, packages provide another level of abstraction for our code and allow us to organize related modules under a single package namespace. It's helpful to think of a package as a module containing other modules. In fact, this is pretty much how Python treats packages. Regardless of whether you import a single, standalone module (i.e., a *.py* file) or a package (i.e., a directory), Python will create a module object in the current namespace. For example, let's import the pycounts package we created in **Chapter 3: How to package a Python** and check its type (recall that this package contains two modules; *pycounts.py* and *plotting.py*):

If you're following on from **Chapter 3: How to package a Python** and created a virtual environment for your pycounts package using conda, as we did in **Section 3.5.1**, be sure to activate that environment before continuing with this chapter by running conda activate pycounts at the command line.

```
>>> import pycounts
>>> type(pycounts)
```

```
module
```

Note that despite importing our pycounts package (which contains two modules), Python still created a single module object. Just as before, we can access the contents of our package via dot notation. For example, we can import the plot_words() function from the plotting module of the pycounts package using the following syntax:

```
>>> from pycounts.plotting import plot_words
>>> type(plot_words)
```

```
function
```

While we get a module object regardless of whether we import a single module (a single *.py* file) or a package (a directory containing one or more *.py* files), one technical difference between a module and a package in Python is that packages are imported as module objects that have a __path__ attribute.

When importing a package or module, Python searches for it in the default list of directories defined in sys.path:

```
>>> import sys
>>> sys.path
```

```
['',
 '/opt/miniconda/base/envs/pycounts/lib/python39.zip',
 '/opt/miniconda/base/envs/pycounts/lib/python3.9',
 '/opt/miniconda/base/envs/pycounts/lib/python3.9/lib-dynload',
 '/opt/miniconda/base/envs/pycounts/lib/python3.9/site-packages']
```

The list of directories shown by sys.path will change depending on how you installed Python and whether or not you're in a virtual environment. The empty string at the start of the list represents the current directory.

But when importing something from a package, Python uses the __path__ attribute of the package to look for that something, rather than the paths in sys.path. For example, let's check the __path__ attribute of the pycounts object:

```
>>> pycounts.__path__
```

```
['/Users/tomasbeuzen/pycounts/src/pycounts']
```

In **Section 3.5.2** we discussed how `poetry`, the tool we're using to develop our `pycounts` package, installs packages in "editable" mode meaning that it installs a link to your package's code on your computer, and that's what we see in the output above. If you install `pycounts` (or any other package) using `pip install` or `conda install` and check its `__path__` attribute you would see a path including a *site-packages/* directory, which is where Python puts installed packages by default, e.g.: `['/opt/miniconda/base/envs/pycounts/lib/python3.9/site-packages/pycounts']`.

We'll talk more about package installation in **Section 4.3**.

What this all means is that when you type `import pycounts.plotting`, Python first searches for a module or package called `pycounts` in the list of search paths defined by `sys.path`. If `pycounts` is a package, it then searches for a `plotting` module or subpackage using `pycounts.__path__` as the search path (rather than `sys.path`). At this point, we're straying into the nuances of Python's import system and digressing from the scope of this book, but interested readers can read more about Python's import system in the Python documentation[4].

Ultimately, the important takeaway message from this section is that packages are a collection of Python modules. They help us better organize and access our code, as well as distribute it to others, as we'll discuss in **Section 4.3**.

4.2 Package structure

With the theory out of the way, we'll now get back to more practical topics in this section; we'll discuss how packages are structured, how we can control their `import` behavior, and how we can include non-code files, like data, into our packages.

4.2.1 Package contents

As we discussed in **Section 4.1**, packages are a way of organizing and accessing a collection of modules. Fundamentally, a package is identified as a directory containing an *__init__.py* file, and a module is a file with a *.py*

---

[4]https://docs.python.org/3/reference/import.html

extension that contains Python code. Below is an example directory structure
of a simple Python package with two modules and a subpackage:

```
pkg
├── __init__.py
├── module1.py
└── subpkg
    ├── __init__.py
    └── module2.py
```

The *__init__.py* tells Python to treat a directory as a package (or subpackage).
It is common for *__init__.py* files to be empty, but they can also contain
helpful initialization code to run when your package is imported, as we'll
discuss in **Section 4.2.4**.

The above structure satisfies the criteria for a Python package, and you would
be able to import content from this package on your local computer if it was
in the current working directory (or if its path had been manually added to
sys.path). But this package lacks the content required to make it installable.

To create an installable package, we need a tool capable of installing and
building packages. Currently the most common tools used for package development are poetry, flit, and setuptools. In this book, we use poetry, but
we'll compare these tools later in **Section 4.3.3**. Regardless of the tool you
use, it will rely on a configuration file(s) that defines the metadata and installation instructions for your package. In a poetry-managed project, that file
is the *pyproject.toml*. It's also good practice to include a README in your
package's root directory to provide high-level information about the package,
and to put the Python code of your package in a *src/* directory (we'll discuss
why this is in **Section 4.2.7**). Thus, the structure for an installable package
looks more like this:

```
pkg
├── src
│   └── pkg
│       ├── __init__.py
│       ├── module1.py
│       └── subpkg
│           ├── __init__.py
│           └── module2.py
├── README.md
└── pyproject.toml
```

The above structure is suitable for a simple package, or one intended solely for
personal use. But most packages include many more bells and whistles than

this, such as detailed documentation, tests, and more, as we saw in **Chapter 3: How to package a Python**. The pycounts package we created in that chapter is a more typical example of a Python package structure:

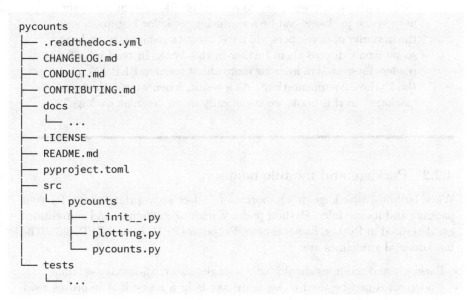

```
pycounts
├── .readthedocs.yml
├── CHANGELOG.md
├── CONDUCT.md
├── CONTRIBUTING.md
├── docs
│   └── ...
├── LICENSE
├── README.md
├── pyproject.toml
├── src
│   └── pycounts
│       ├── __init__.py
│       ├── plotting.py
│       └── pycounts.py
└── tests
    └── ...
```

Not all of this content will be included in the version of your package that you install or distribute to others. Typically, it's just the Python code (in the *src/* directory) that forms the installable version of your package (but we'll show how you can specify additional content to include in **Section 4.2.5**). The rest of the content, like documentation and tests, exists to support development, and this content is not needed by the users of your package, so it's usually shared (if desired) via a collaborative medium like GitHub, where other developers can access and contribute to it.

The package structure described in this section is technically called a "regular package" in Python, and it is what the vast majority of Python packages and developers use. However, Python also supports a second type of package known as a "namespace package". Namespace packages are a way of splitting a single Python package across multiple directories. Unlike regular packages, where all contents live in the same directory hierarchy, namespace packages can be formed from directories in different locations on a file system and do not contain an *__init__.py* file.

The main reason a developer might want to use a namespace package is if they wish to develop, install, and distribute portions of a package separately, or if they want to combine packages that reside on different locations on their file system. However, namespace packages can be a confusing topic for beginners and the majority of developers will never create a namespace package so we won't discuss them further in this book. Instead we refer readers interested in learning more about them to PEP 420[5] and the Python documentation[6]. As a result, when we use the term "package" in this book, we specifically mean "regular package".

4.2.2 Package and module names

When building a package, it's important to select appropriate names for your package and its modules. Python package naming guidelines and conventions are described in Python Enhancement Proposal (PEP) 8[7] and PEP 423[8]. The fundamental guidelines are:

- Packages and modules should have a single, short, all-lowercase name.
- Underscores can be used to separate words in a name if it improves readability, but their use is typically discouraged.

In terms of the actual name chosen for a module or package, it may be helpful to consider the following "three M's":

1. **Meaningful**: the name should reflect the functionality of the package.
2. **Memorable**: the name should be easy for users to find, remember, and relate to other relevant packages.
3. **Manageable**: remember that users of your package will access its contents/namespace via dot notation. Make it as quick and easy as possible for them to do this by keeping your names short and sweet. For example, imagine if we called our `pycounts` package something like `wordcountingpackage`. Every time a user wanted to access the `plot_words()` function from the `plotting` module, they'd have to write this: `from wordcountingpackage.plotting import plot_words()` — yikes!

Finally, you should always check PyPI[9] and other popular hosting sites like

---

[5]https://www.python.org/dev/peps/pep-0420/
[6]https://docs.python.org/3/reference/import.html#namespace-packages
[7]https://www.python.org/dev/peps/pep-0008/
[8]https://www.python.org/dev/peps/pep-0423/
[9]https://pypi.org

GitHub, GitLab, BitBucket, etc., to make sure that your chosen package name is not already in use.

FIGURE 4.1: Keep package names meaningful, memorable, and manageable.

4.2.3 Intra-package references

When building packages of multiple modules, it is common to want to use code from one module in another. For example, consider the following package structure:

```
src
└── package
    ├── __init__.py
    ├── moduleA.py
    ├── moduleB.py
    └── subpackage
        ├── __init__.py
        └── moduleC.py
```

A developer may want to import code from moduleA in moduleB. This is an "intra-package reference" and can be accomplished via an "absolute" or "relative" import.

Absolute imports use the package name in an absolute context. Relative imports use dots to indicate from where the relative import should begin. A single dot indicates an import relative to the current package (or subpackage), additional dots can be used to move further up the packaging hierarchy, one level per dot after the first dot.

Table 4.1 shows some practical examples of absolute and relative imports, based on the package structure shown previously.

TABLE 4.1: Demonstration of absolute and relative intra-package imports.

	Absolute	Relative
Import from `moduleA` in `moduleB`	`from package.moduleA import XXX`	`from .moduleA import XXX`
Import from `moduleA` in `moduleC`	`from package.moduleA import XXX`	`from ..moduleA import XXX`
Import from `moduleC` in `moduleA`	`from pack-age.subpackage.moduleC import XXX`	`from .subpackage.moduleC import XXX`

While the choice here mostly comes down to personal preference, PEP 8[10] recommends using absolute imports because they are explicit.

4.2.4   The init file

Earlier we discussed how an `__init__.py` file is used to tell Python that the directory containing the `__init__.py` file is a package. The `__init__.py` file can be, and often is, left empty and only used for the purpose of identifying a directory as a package. However, it can also be used to add objects to the package's namespace, provide documentation, and/or run other initialization code.

We'll demonstrate this functionality using the `pycounts` packages we developed in **Chapter 3: How to package a Python**. Consider the `__init__.py` of our package:

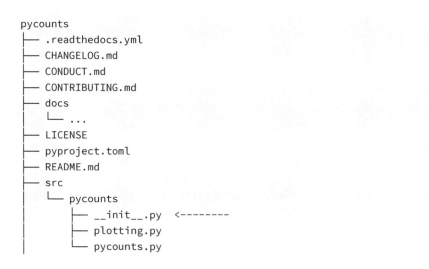

```
pycounts
├── .readthedocs.yml
├── CHANGELOG.md
├── CONDUCT.md
├── CONTRIBUTING.md
├── docs
│   └── ...
├── LICENSE
├── pyproject.toml
├── README.md
├── src
│   └── pycounts
│       ├── __init__.py   <--------
│       ├── plotting.py
│       └── pycounts.py
```

---

[10]`https://www.python.org/dev/peps/pep-0008/`

```
└── tests
    └── ...
```

When a package is imported, the __init__.py file is executed, and any objects it defines are bound to the package's namespace. As an example, in Python packaging, it's convention to define a package's version in two places:

1. In the package's configuration file, *pyproject.toml*, as we saw in **Section 3.5.2**.
2. In the package's __init__.py file using the __version__ attribute, so users can quickly check the version of your package they are using, with code like:

```
>>> import pycounts
>>> pycounts.__version__
```

```
0.1.0
```

Sometimes you'll see the version number hard-coded in the __init__.py file, like __version__ = "0.1.0". But this means you have to remember to update the version in two places anytime you want to make a new version of your package — __init__.py and *pyproject.toml* (we'll discuss versioning in **Chapter 7: Releasing and versioning**). Instead, it's better to have your package version defined only in *pyproject.toml*, and then read programmatically in the __init__.py file using the importlib.metadata.version() function, which reads a package's version from its installed metadata (i.e., the *pyproject.toml* file).

The py-pkgs-cookiecutter we used to create our pycounts package (**Section 3.2.2**) already populated our __init__.py file with this code for us:

```
# read version from installed package
from importlib.metadata import version
__version__ = version("pycounts")
```

Because any objects defined in the __init__.py get bound to the package's namespace upon import, the __version__ variable is accessible from our package's namespace as we saw earlier.

Another common use case of the __init__.py file is to control the import behavior of a package. For example, there are currently only two main functions that users will commonly use from our pycounts package: py-

counts.count_words() and plotting.plot_words(). Users have to type the full
path to these functions to import them:

```
from pycounts.pycounts import count_words
from pycounts.plotting import plot_words
```

We could make life easier for our users by importing these core functions in
pycounts's *__init__.py* file, which would bind them to the package namespace.
For example, the code below, added to the *__init__.py* file, imports our core
functions pycounts.count_words() and plotting.plot_words():

```
# read version from installed package
from importlib.metadata import version
__version__ = version(__name__)

# populate package namespace
from pycounts.pycounts import count_words
from pycounts.plotting import plot_words
```

If you're following along and developing the pycounts package
in this book, and tried installing it from TestPyPI or PyPI in
Section 3.10, it will no longer be installed in "editable mode"
and so won't reflect any changes you make to the source code.
You'll have to run poetry install to see your changes and put
your package back in editable mode (which is the mode you want
for development).

The functions are now bound to the pycounts namespace, so users can access
them like this:

```
>>> import pycounts
>>> pycounts.count_words
```

```
<function count_words>
```

Ultimately, the *__init__.py* file can be used to customize how your package
and its contents are imported. It's an interesting exercise to visit large Python

packages, such as NumPy[11], pandas[12], or scikitlearn[13], to see the kinds of initialization code they run in their *__init__.py* files.

4.2.5   Including non-code files in a package

Consider again the full structure of our pycounts package:

```
pycounts
├── .readthedocs.yml
├── CHANGELOG.md
├── CONDUCT.md
├── CONTRIBUTING.md
├── docs
│   ├── changelog.md
│   ├── conduct.md
│   ├── conf.py
│   ├── contributing.md
│   ├── example.ipynb
│   ├── index.md
│   ├── make.bat
│   ├── Makefile
│   └── requirements.txt
├── LICENSE
├── README.md
├── poetry.lock
├── pyproject.toml
├── src
│   └── pycounts
│       ├── __init__.py
│       └── pycounts.py
└── tests
    ├── einstein.text
    └── test_pycounts.py
```

The installable version of your package that you distribute to others will typically only contain the Python code in the *src/* directory. The rest of the content exists to support development of the package and is not needed by users to actually use the package. This content is typically shared by the developer by some other means, such as GitHub, so that other developers can access and contribute to it if they wish.

However, it is possible to include arbitrary additional content in your package

---

[11]https://github.com/numpy/numpy/blob/main/numpy/__init__.py
[12]https://github.com/pandas-dev/pandas/blob/master/pandas/__init__.py
[13]https://github.com/scikit-learn/scikit-learn/blob/main/sklearn/__init__.py

that will get installed by users, along with the usual Python code. The method of doing this varies depending on what packaging tool you're using, but with poetry, you can specify the extra content you wish to include in your package using the include parameter under the [tool.poetry] table in *pyproject.toml*. For example, if we wanted to include our *tests/* directory and *CHANGELOG.md* file to our installable package distribution, we would add the following to *pyproject.toml*:

```
[tool.poetry]
name = "pycounts"
version = "0.1.0"
description = "Calculate word counts in a text file!"
authors = ["Tomas Beuzen"]
license = "MIT"
readme = "README.md"
include = ["tests/*", "CHANGELOG.md"]
```

...rest of file hidden...

Most developers won't ship additional content with their package like this, preferring to share it via a service like GitHub, but there are certainly use cases for doing so — for example, if you're sharing a package privately within an organization, you may wish to ship everything with your package (documentation, tests, etc.).

4.2.6   Including data in a package

One type of non-code that developers do commonly want to include in a package is data. There are several reasons why a developer might want to include data in their package:

1. It's required to use some of the package's functionality.
2. To provide example data to help demonstrate the functionality of the package.
3. As a method of distributing and versioning a data file(s).
4. If the package is being used to bundle up a reproducible data analysis and it's important to keep the code and data together.

Regardless of the use case, there are two typical ways to include data in a Python package:

1. Include the raw data as part of the installable package, and provide code to help users load it (if required). This option is well-suited to smaller data files, or for data that the package absolutely depends on.

2. Include scripts as part of the package that download the data from an external source. This option is suited to large data files, or ones that a user may only need optionally.

We'll demonstrate option 1 above with an example. Our pycounts package helps users calculate words counts in text files. To demonstrate our package's functionality to new users, it might be helpful to add an example text file to our package for them to practice with. For our package, we'll add a text file of the novel *Flatland*, by Edwin Abbott (Abbott, 1884) (available online[14]).

To include this data in our package, we need to do two things:

1. Include the raw *.txt* file in our package.
2. Include code to help a user access the data.

We'll start by creating a new *data* subpackage in our *src/pycounts/* directory, where you should download and place the linked *Flatland* novel as *flatland.txt*. We'll also create a new module *datasets.py* in our package that we'll shortly populate with code to help users load data. Our pycounts directory structure now looks like this:

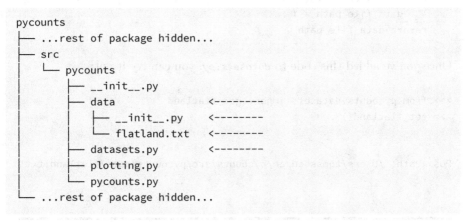

Now we need to add some Python code to *datasets.py* to help users load the example data. The recommended way to access data files in a package is using the importlib.resources module[15]. The main function of our pycounts package, pycounts.count_words() requires users to pass a file path to the text file they want to count words in. So, we should write a function in our new *datasets.py* that returns the path to the example *flatland.txt* file to the user. The importlib.resources.path() function can help us do that. You can read about this function in the Python documentation[16]; it is used in a with

---

[14]https://www.gutenberg.org/ebooks/97

[15]https://docs.python.org/3/library/importlib.html#module-importlib.resources

[16]https://docs.python.org/3/library/importlib.html#importlib.resources.path

statement and requires two parameters, the location of the subpackage the data is in ("pycounts.data") and the name of the data file to access within that subpackage ("flatland.txt"). The code below, which we'll add to *datasets.py*, demonstrates its usage:

```python
from importlib import resources

def get_flatland():
    """Get path to example "Flatland" [1]_ text file.

    Returns
    -------
    pathlib.PosixPath
        Path to file.

    References
    ----------
    .. [1] E. A. Abbott, "Flatland", Seeley & Co., 1884.
    """
    with resources.path("pycounts.data", "flatland.txt") as f:
        data_file_path = f
    return data_file_path
```

Once you've added this code to *datasets.py*, you can try it out:

```python
>>> from pycounts.datasets import get_flatland
>>> get_flatland()


PosixPath('/Users/tomasbeuzen/pycounts/src/pycounts/data/flatland.txt')
```

If you're following along and developing the pycounts package in this book, and tried installing it from TestPyPI or PyPI in **Section 3.10**, it will no longer be installed in "editable mode" and so won't reflect any changes you make to the source code. You'll have to run poetry install to see your changes and put your package back in editable mode (which is the mode you want for development).

A user can directly use this path in the pycounts function count_words() as follows:

```
>>> from pycounts.pycounts import count_words
>>> from pycounts.datasets import get_flatland
>>> flatland_path = get_flatland()
>>> count_words(flatland_path)
```

```
Counter({'the': 2244, 'of': 1597, 'to': 1078, 'and': 1074,
'a': 902, 'i': 706, 'in': 698, 'that': 486, ... })
```

This is just one example of how we can include data as part of our package and expose it to a user. The importlib.resources module can be used to load any kind of data in different ways (as a path, as a string, as a binary file, etc.). If you're developing a package that includes user-facing data, we recommend taking a look at the importlib.resources documentation[17], as well as the "datasets" modules included in larger Python libraries such as scikit-learn[18], torchvision[19], or statsmodels[20] to learn more.

4.2.7 The source layout

When describing and defining package structure throughout this book, we have been nesting our package's Python code inside a *src/* directory, as in the example structure below. This layout is called the "src"/"source" layout for obvious reasons.

```
pkg
├── ...
├── src
│   └── pkg
│       ├── __init__.py
│       ├── module1.py
│       └── subpkg
│           ├── __init__.py
│           └── module2.py
└── ...
```

However, nesting a package's code in a *src/* directory is not required to build

---

[17]https://docs.python.org/3/library/importlib.html#module-importlib.resources
[18]https://github.com/scikit-learn/scikit-learn/tree/main/sklearn/datasets
[19]https://github.com/pytorch/vision/tree/main/torchvision/datasets
[20]https://github.com/statsmodels/statsmodels/tree/main/statsmodels/datasets

a package, and it's also common to see packages without it. We'll call this the "non-src" layout and show an example below.

```
pkg
├── ...
├── pkg
│   ├── __init__.py
│   ├── module1.py
│   └── subpkg
│       ├── __init__.py
│       └── module2.py
└── ...
```

In general, we recommend using the "src" layout over the "non-src" layout (and so does the Python Packaging Authority[21]) because it has several advantages when it comes to developing and distributing installable Python packages. We list a few of these below:

1. For developers using a testing framework like `pytest`, a "src" layout forces you to install your package before it can be tested. Most developers would agree that you would want to test your package as it will be installed by users, rather than as it currently exists on your own machine. The problem with a "non-src" layout is that Python can `import` your package even if it is not installed. This is because in most cases the first place Python searches when running `import` is the current directory (check this by importing `sys` and running `sys.path[0]`). Without a "src" folder, Python will find your package as it exists in the current directory and import it, rather than using it as it would be installed on a user's machine. There are plenty of horror stories of developers uploading broken distributions to PyPI because they were testing their code as it existed on their machine rather than as it would be installed by users. This issue is described in detail in Ionel Cristian Mărieș' Packaging a Python Library[22] and Hynek Schlawack's Testing and Packaging[23] excellent blog posts for those interested.

2. A "src" layout leads to cleaner editable installs of your package. Recall from **Section 3.5.2** that when developing a package, it's common to install it in editable mode (the default when running `poetry install`). This adds the path to your project's Python code to the `sys.path` list so that changes to your source code are

---

[21]https://packaging.python.org/tutorials/packaging-projects/
[22]https://blog.ionelmc.ro/2014/05/25/python-packaging/
[23]https://hynek.me/articles/testing-packaging/

immediately available when you `import` it, without needing to reinstall. With a "src" layout that path looks something like this:

```
'/Users/tomasbeuzen/pycounts/src'
```

In contrast, a "non-src" layout will add your project's root to `sys.path` (there is no "src" directory to provide a layer of separation):

```
'/Users/tomasbeuzen/pycounts/'
```

There's usually a lot more than just Python code at that path. There could be test modules, scratch code, data files, documentation, example scripts, etc., all of which are now potentially importable in your development workflow!

3. Finally, "src" is generally a universally recognized location for source code, making it easier for others to quickly navigate the contents of your package.

Ultimately, while you can certainly use a "non-src layout" to develop a package, using a "src" layout will typically reduce the chance of things breaking during development and distribution.

4.3 Package distribution and installation

In this section, we won't be writing any code, but rather we will discuss theory related to package distribution and installation for those interested. If that's not you, feel free to skip to **Section 4.4**.

As we saw in **Chapter 3: How to package a Python**, the typical workflow for developing and distributing a Python packages is as follows:

1. A *developer* creates a Python package on their machine.
2. The *developer* uses a tool like `poetry` to build a distribution from that package.
3. The *developer* shares the distribution, usually by uploading to a online repository like PyPI[24].

---

[24]https://pypi.org

4. A *user* uses an installation tool like `pip` to download the distribution and install it on their machine.
5. (Optional) *Users* provide feedback to the developer about the package (identify bugs, request features, etc.) and the cycle repeats.

This workflow is illustrated in Fig. 4.2.

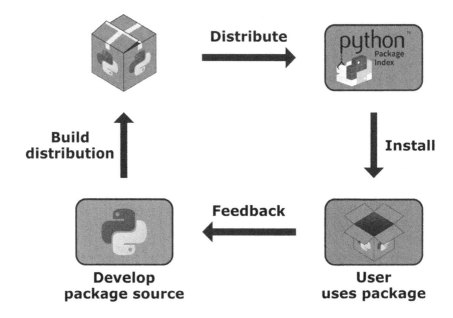

FIGURE 4.2: The Python package cycle.

To build up an intuition of the steps in this process, we'll begin at the user-end, and discuss how packages are installed. We'll then work our way backwards to better understand what distributions are and how they're made.

4.3.1 Package installation

To be installed, a package needs to generate two directories:

1. *{package}*: a directory of the package's source files (i.e., modules and subpackages).
2. *{package}-{version}*.`dist-info`: a directory of files containing information about the package, such as a metadata file with information such as the package's author and what versions of Python it supports (METADATA), a license file (LICENSE), a file specifying

what tool was used to install the package (INSTALLER), and more. These files are described in detail in PEP 427[25].

We'll talk about how these directories are actually built shortly, but for now, we'll talk about installation. When you install a package with an installer like pip the above directories are copied into the *site-packages/* directory of your Python installation, which is one of the default places Python looks when importing a package. The exact path to the *site-packages/* directory varies depending on your operating system, how you installed Python, and whether you're using a virtual environment. You can check the path using the sys.path variable. The below paths are for a MacOS, with Python installed via Miniconda[26], and with a virtual environments called pycounts activated:

```
>>> import sys
>>> sys.path
```

```
['',
 '/opt/miniconda/base/envs/pycounts/lib/python39.zip',
 '/opt/miniconda/base/envs/pycounts/lib/python3.9',
 '/opt/miniconda/base/envs/pycounts/lib/python3.9/lib-dynload',
 '/opt/miniconda/base/envs/pycounts/lib/python3.9/site-packages']
```

If you navigate to the *site-packages/* directory you will see examples of the *{package}* and *{package}-{version}.dist-info* directories for each package you have installed. For example, if we were to pip install the pycounts package we uploaded to PyPI in **Section 3.10**, we would see the following in our *site-packages* folder:

```
'/opt/miniconda/base/lib/python3.9/site-packages/pycounts'
├── __init__.py
├── __pycache__
├── plotting.py
└── pycounts.py
```

```
/opt/miniconda/base/lib/python3.9/site-packages/pycounts-0.1.0.dist-info
├── INSTALLER
├── LICENSE
├── METADATA
├── RECORD
```

---

[25]https://www.python.org/dev/peps/pep-0427/#the-dist-info-directory
[26]https://docs.conda.io/en/latest/miniconda.html

├─ REQUESTED
└─ WHEEL

So the question is, how do we provide the *{package}* and *{package}-{version}.dist-info* directories necessary to install our package? There are two options:

1. Create a single archive of all our package source code, metadata, and instructions on how to create the *{package}* and *{package}-{version}.dist-info* directories, and then share that archive with users. This is called a source distribution or sdist. To install your package from an sdist, a user needs to download the archive, unpack it, and use the included build instructions to build it into the *{package}* and *{package}-{version}.dist-info* directories on their own computer (we'll talk about how these directories are "built" in **Section 4.3.2**). Finally, the package is installed by copying these directories to the *site-packages/* directory.
2. Build the *{package}* and *{package}-{version}.dist-info* directories on our own machine, compress them into a single file, and share them with users. This single file is called a wheel. A user just needs to download the wheel and extract the contents to the *site-packages/* folder; no build step is necessary.

pip install can handle installation from an sdist or a wheel, but distributing your package to users as a wheel (option 2) certainly seems preferable; everything has already been done on the developer's side and installation just involves downloading the distribution and copying it to the appropriate location on a user's computer. This is why wheels are the preferred distribution format for Python packages. In fact, when you run pip install <some-package>, it will always prioritize installing the specified package from a wheel (if it exists).

At this point you might be wondering why we bother with sdists at all. The reason is that wheels aren't always available to users. Some Python packages contain "extensions" written in other languages, such as C/C++, because they offer functionality and performance enhancements. While Python is typically referred to as an interpreted language (i.e., your Python code is translated to machine code as it is executed), languages such as C/C++ require compilation by a compiler program before they can be used (i.e., your code must be translated into "machine code" *before* it can be executed). Compilation is platform-specific. Thus, if a developer wanted to provide wheels of a package that included extensions in another language, they would have to generate one wheel for each platform they wanted to support (e.g., MacOS-arm64, MacOS-x86, Win-32, Win-amd64, etc.). For this reason, sdists are usually provided with wheels; if a wheel isn't available for a user's particular platform, they will still be able to build the package from the sdist (which would require that they have the appropriate compiling program(s)).

As an example, the popular numpy package contains extensions written in C, so its wheels are platform-specific. Wheels have a specific naming convention (described in PEP 427[27]), which includes the name of the platform they support; if you look at numpy's distributions on PyPi[28], you'll see wheels for common platforms, as well as an sdist at the bottom of the list.

Wheels specific to a platform are known as "platform wheels". However, the vast majority of Python packages use pure Python code (i.e., they don't include extensions written in other languages), and so don't need to worry about generating platform wheels. Most developers and readers of this book will only ever generate one wheel for their package: a "universal wheel" (compatible with Python 2 and 3) or a "pure Python wheel" (compatible with either Python 2 or 3). The build tool you use to make your distributions will handle wheel creation for you (as we'll talk about in the next section), so it's not something you need to worry about, but it's interesting to know these things!

4.3.2 Building sdists and wheels

In the previous section we talked about how packages need to generate *{package}* and *{package}-{version}.dist-info* folders to be installed, and how a wheel is a single archive containing these files. So how exactly do we build a wheel?

In a nutshell the build process involves: 1. Developer builds the package source into an sdist{distribution!sdists}; 2. Developer or user builds a wheel from the sdist; 3. Users installs the wheel{distribution!wheel}.

The build steps here are where packaging tools like poetry, flit, or setuptools come in. These tools provide the code required to build sdists and wheels. Recall the *pyproject.toml* file poetry uses to manage package development. One table in that file we did not talk about when we introduced the file in **Section 3.5.2** is [build-system]:

```
...other file content hidden...

[build-system]
requires = ["poetry-core>=1.0.0"]
build-backend = "poetry.core.masonry.api"
```

This table specifies the tools required to build the sdist and wheel for a package (requires) and where the functions that actually do the build are located

---

[27]https://www.python.org/dev/peps/pep-0427/
[28]https://pypi.org/project/numpy/#files

in a build-tool's library (`build-backend`). For example, the table above shows that the `poetry-core` library is required to build our package, and that the building functions are located in `poetry.core.masonry.api`. If you take a look at the source code of `poetry-core`'s `poetry.core.masonry.api` module[29], you'll see functions like `build_wheel()` and `build_sdist()`. The exact building mechanics are beyond the scope of this book, so we wont go into detail about how they work. However, as a packaging book, it would be remiss not to mention that the ability to specify the build tools required to make sdists and wheels of a package is a relatively new development in the packaging ecosystem. This functionality was introduced in PEP 517[30] and PEP 518[31], to remove the dependency of the packaging system on legacy tools. These PEPs are an interesting read for those keen on digging into more of the low-level details of building and installing package distributions.

4.3.3   Packaging tools

The focus of this book is on workflows and tools that make packaging accessible and efficient. `poetry` is one of those tools; it abstracts the lower-level details of package development away from the developer so they can focus on writing code. `poetry` is completely configured by a single *pyproject.toml* file and has intuitive commands to install a package (`poetry install`), manage dependencies (`poetry add`), build distributions (`poetry build`), and publish those distributions to a repository like PyPI (`poetry publish`).

An alternative modern packaging tool is `flit`. `flit` is essentially a stripped-down version of `poetry`. It is also managed by a *pyproject.toml* file and provides commands similar to `poetry` to help install a package (`flit install`), build distributions (`flit build`), and publish those distributions to a repository like PyPI (`flit publish`). The main difference between `flit` and `poetry` is that `flit` doesn't automatically manage the dependencies of your project like `poetry` does; you have to manually add dependencies and their version specifications to *pyproject.toml*. As a result, we prefer `poetry` because it means there's one less thing to worry about!

The downside of `poetry` and `flit` is that, at the time of writing, they only support pure Python packages and not packages that contain extensions written in other languages, which we discussed in **Section 4.3.1**. This is completely fine for the vast majority of developers. However, for those looking to build more advanced packages that include non-Python code, `setuptools` is the preferred option. For a long time, `setuptools` was the default build tool for Python packages so it is still used by many projects that have been around for a while. `setuptools` require a little more expertise to configure than `poetry` or

---

[29]https://github.com/python-poetry/poetry-core/blob/master/src/poetry/core/masonry/api.py
[30]https://www.python.org/dev/peps/pep-0517/
[31]https://www.python.org/dev/peps/pep-0518/

flit, as you can read more about in the documentation[32], so we prefer poetry or flit for packaging projects where possible.

4.3.4   Package repositories

In **Chapter 3: How to package a Python**, we released our pycounts package to the Python Package Index (PyPI[33]) and discussed how PyPI is the main repository for Python packages. Even if you've never heard of PyPI, if you've ever run pip install <some-package> you've installed packages from there. If you're interested in sharing your work publicly, PyPI is probably where you'll release your package, however, it is not the only option.

The Anaconda[34] and conda-forge[35] repositories are the next most popular software repositories for Python packages. Packages on these repositories can be installed from the command line using conda install (we installed the conda tool in **Section 2.2.1**). The main differences between PyPI and these repositories is that they can host non-Python software (as opposed to PyPI which only hosts Python software), and conda packages are binaries (there is never a need to have to build a package or its dependencies from an sdist). As a result, packages that depend on non-Python code are usually released to Anaconda or conda-forge. Even for packages that are pure Python, developers sometimes still also create a conda package and upload to Anaconda or conda-forge to cater to users who are using conda as a package manager rather than pip. For those interested, Anaconda provides a helpful tutorial[36] to help convert packages on PyPI to conda packages, but for most readers of this book, building sdist and wheel distributions and sharing them on PyPI will be enough.

In some cases, you may want to release your package to a private repository (for example, for internal use by your company only). There are many private repository options for Python packages. Companies like Anaconda[37], PyDist[38], and GemFury[39] are all examples that offer (typically paid) private Python package repository hosting. You can also set up your own server on a dedicated machine or cloud service — as discussed in this article[40]. You can also choose to host your package on GitHub (or equivalent), and forego releasing to a dedicated software repository. pip install supports installing a package directly from a GitHub repository you have access to, as discussed

---

[32]https://setuptools.readthedocs.io/en/latest/userguide/index.html

[33]https://pypi.org/

[34]https://anaconda.org/anaconda/repo

[35]https://conda-forge.org

[36]https://docs.conda.io/projects/conda-build/en/latest/user-guide/tutorials/build-pkgs-skeleton.html

[37]https://docs.anaconda.com/

[38]https://pydist.com/

[39]https://gemfury.com/

[40]https://medium.com/swlh/how-to-install-a-private-pypi-server-on-aws-76993e45c610

in the documentation[41]. You can `pip install` from a repository branch, a specific commit, or a tag. For example, we tagged a release of v0.1.0 of our `pycounts` package on GitHub in **Section 3.9**. Others could now install our package directly from GitHub using the following command:

```
$ pip install git+https://github.com/TomasBeuzen/pycounts.git@v0.1.0
```

Installing from GitHub can be useful for users wanting a version of your package not yet available on PyPI (for example, a development version), or if you want to host your package in a private repository and only share it with a select few collaborators. In general though, we don't recommend GitHub for sharing Python packages to a wide audience as the vast majority of Python users do not install packages from GitHub, and dedicated software repositories like PyPI provide better discoverability, ease of installation, and a stamp of authenticity.

4.4   Version control

In **Section 4.2.6** we made an important change to our `pycounts` package by adding a new `datasets` module and some example data. We will make a new release of our package in **Chapter 7: Releasing and versioning** that incorporates this change. So, if you're following along building the `pycounts` package yourself and using version control, commit these changes to your local and remote repositories using the commands below. If you're not building the `pycounts` package or not using version control, you can skip to the next chapter.

```
$ git add src/pycounts/datasets.py src/pycounts/data
$ git commit -m "feat: add example data and datasets module"
$ git push
```

5

Testing

Testing is an important part of Python package development but one that is often neglected due to the perceived additional workload. However, the reality is quite the opposite! Introducing formal, automated testing into your workflow can have several benefits:

1. **Fewer bugs:** you're explicitly constructing and testing your code from the viewpoint of a developer and a user.
2. **Better code structure:** writing tests forces you to structure and organize your code so that it's easier to test and understand.
3. **Easier development:** formal tests will help you and others add features to your code without breaking tried-and-tested existing functionality.

Section 3.7 briefly introduced testing in Python package development. This chapter now goes into more detail about how to write tests, different types of tests (unit tests, regression tests, integration tests), and code coverage.

5.1 Testing workflow

In general, the goal of testing is to check that your code produces the results you expect it to. You probably already conduct informal tests of your code in your current workflow. In a typical workflow, we write code, run it in a Python session to see if it's working as we expect, make changes, repeat. This is sometimes called "manual testing" or "exploratory testing" and is common in the early stages of development of your code. But when developing code you intend to package up, reuse, and potentially share with others, you'll need to test it in a more formal and reproducible way.

In Python, tests are usually written using an `assert` statement, which checks the truth of a given expression, and returns a user-defined error message if the expression is false. To demonstrate this process, imagine we want to create a function called `count_letters()` that counts the number of letters in a string. We come up with the following code as a first version of that function:

```
def count_letters(text):
    """Count letters in a string."""
    return len(text)
```

We can write some tests for that function using the `assert` statement to check it's working as we expect it to. For example we would expect our function to calculate five letters in the string "Hello" and ten letters in the string "Hello world":

```
>>> assert count_letters("Hello") == 5, "'Hello' should have 5 letters"
>>> assert count_letters("Hello world") == 10, "'Hello world' should \
                                       have 10 letters"
```

If we ran the above `assert` statements, the first would pass without error, but the second would raise an error:

```
AssertionError: 'Hello world' should have 10 letters
```

What went wrong? When we call `len()` on a string, it counts all the characters in the string, including the spaces. So, we need to go back to our `count_letters()` function and remove spaces before counting letters. One way we can do this is by using the `.replace()` method to replace spaces with an empty string "" (i.e., nothing):

```
def count_letters(text):
    """Count letters in a string."""
    return len(text.replace(" ", ""))
```

Now our previous `assert` statements should both pass. This process we just went through roughly followed the typical testing workflow of:

1. Write a test.
2. Write the code to be tested.
3. Test the code.
4. Refactor code (make small changes).
5. Repeat.

This workflow is illustrated in Fig. 5.1.

In our earlier demonstration with the `count_letters()` function, we swapped steps 1 and 2; we wrote the first version of our function's code before we wrote our tests, and this is a common workflow too. However, you can see how it might have been beneficial to write the tests (or at least think about them)

Write code **Test code**

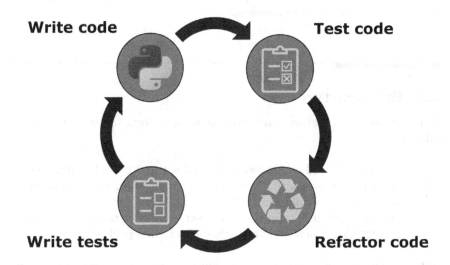

Write tests **Refactor code**

FIGURE 5.1: The testing workflow.

before writing the code; if we knew we were testing text with a space in it, we might have included that in our function in the first place.

Writing your tests before your code is known as "test-driven development", and advocates of this approach suggest that it helps you better understand the code you need to write, prevent bugs, and ultimately save you time. However in practice, writing your tests first or last doesn't seem to have a significant impact on overall development time (Fucci et al., 2016). Regardless of when you choose to formally write your tests, all developers should at least think about the specifications of their code before they write it. What might the inputs look like? What will the output look like? Are there any edge cases[1] to consider? Taking a moment to consider and write down these specifications will help you write code effectively and efficiently.

Ultimately, the testing workflow is all about working incrementally and iteratively. The idea is to make small changes to your code as you add features or identify bugs, test it, write more tests, repeat. Managing and executing such a workflow manually like we did above would clearly be inefficient. Instead, a test framework is typically used to help manage the testing workflow in an efficient, automated, and reproducible way. `pytest` is one of the most common test frameworks for Python packages. We used it to help test our `pycounts` package in **Section 3.7.2**. In the rest of this chapter, we'll continue to explore

---

[1]https://en.wikipedia.org/wiki/Edge_case

how `pytest` can be used to test a package and will demonstrate concepts by writing tests for the `pycounts` package.

5.2   Test structure

To use `pytest` as a testing framework, it expects tests to be structured as follows:

1. Tests are defined as functions prefixed with `test_` and contain one or more statements that `assert` code produces an expected result or raises a particular error.
2. Tests are put in files of the form *test_*.py* or **_test.py*, and are usually placed in a directory called *tests/* in a package's root.

Tests can be executed using the command `pytest` at the command line and pointing it to the directory your tests live in (i.e., `pytest tests/`). `pytest` will find all files of the form *test_*.py* or **_test.py* in that directory and its subdirectories, and execute any functions with names prefixed with `test_`.

As an example, consider the structure of the `pycounts` package we developed in **Chapter 3: How to package a Python**:

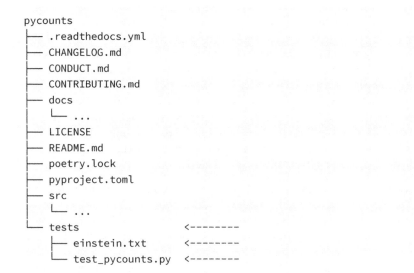

```
pycounts
├── .readthedocs.yml
├── CHANGELOG.md
├── CONDUCT.md
├── CONTRIBUTING.md
├── docs
│   └── ...
├── LICENSE
├── README.md
├── poetry.lock
├── pyproject.toml
├── src
│   └── ...
└── tests                    <--------
    ├── einstein.txt         <--------
    └── test_pycounts.py     <--------
```

The file *einstein.txt* is a text file we created in **Section 3.7.1** to use in our tests. It includes a quote from Albert Einstein:

"Insanity is doing the same thing over and over and expecting different results."

The file `test_pycounts.py` is where the tests we want to run with `pytest` should be. That file contains the following test we wrote in **Section 3.7.2**, using the format expected by `pytest`, a function prefixed with `test_` that includes an `assert` statement.

```python
from pycounts.pycounts import count_words
from collections import Counter

def test_count_words():
    """Test word counting from a file."""
    expected = Counter({'insanity': 1, 'is': 1, 'doing': 1,
                        'the': 1, 'same': 1, 'thing': 1,
                        'over': 2, 'and': 2, 'expecting': 1,
                        'different': 1, 'results': 1})
    actual = count_words("tests/einstein.txt")
    assert actual == expected, "Einstein quote counted incorrectly!"
```

To use `pytest` to run this test it should first be installed as a development dependency of your package. If using `poetry` as a packaging tool, as we do in this book, that can be done with the following command:

If you're following on from **Chapter 3: How to package a Python** and created a virtual environment for your `pycounts` package using `conda`, as we did in **Section 3.5.1**, be sure to activate that environment before continuing with this chapter by running `conda activate pycounts` at the command line.

```
$ poetry add --dev pytest
```

With `pytest` installed, we use the following command from our root package directory to run our test:

```
$ pytest tests/


========================= test session starts =========================
...
collected 1 item

tests/test_pycounts.py .                                         [100%]

========================= 1 passed in 0.01s =========================
```

The output of `pytest` provides some basic system information, along with how many tests were run and what percentage passed. If a test fails, it will output the traceback of the error, so you can see exactly which test failed and why. In the next section, we'll go into more detail about how to write different kinds of tests in `pytest`.

5.3   Writing tests

There are several kinds of tests commonly used to test Python packages: unit tests, integration tests, and regression tests. In this section, we'll explore and demonstrate what these tests are and how to write them in `pytest`.

5.3.1   Unit tests

Unit tests are the most common type of test you will write. A unit test verifies that an independent unit of code (e.g., a Python function) is working as expected in a particular situation. It will typically comprise:

1. Some data to test the code with (called a "fixture"). The fixture is typically a small or simple version of the type of data the function will typically process.
2. The *actual* result that the code produces given the fixture.
3. The *expected* result of the test, which is compared to the *actual* result, typically using an `assert` statement.

The `test_count_words()` function of our `pycounts` package is an example of a unit test. Recall that our `count_words()` function can be used to calculate words counts in a text file. To test it, we created a small, sample text file called *einstein.txt* (our fixture), which contains the following quote:

> *"Insanity is doing the same thing over and over and expecting different results."*

The result of our `count_words()` function using this fixture is the *actual* result. The fixture is small enough that we can count the words by hand, and that forms our *expected* result. Thus the unit test currently in our `test_pycounts.py` looks as follows:

```python
from pycounts.pycounts import count_words
from collections import Counter

def test_count_words():
    """Test word counting from a file."""
    expected = Counter({'insanity': 1, 'is': 1, 'doing': 1,
                        'the': 1, 'same': 1, 'thing': 1,
                        'over': 2, 'and': 2, 'expecting': 1,
                        'different': 1, 'results': 1})
    actual = count_words("tests/einstein.txt")
    assert actual == expected, "Einstein quote counted incorrectly!"
```

A pytest test function can actually include multiple `assert` statements and if any of the included `assert` functions fail, the whole test will fail. As an example of a unit test with multiple `assert` statements, we'll write a new test in our `test_pycounts.py` file for the `plot_words()` function of our `pycounts.plotting` module. We developed the `plot_words()` function in **Section 3.6** and show it below:

```python
import matplotlib.pyplot as plt

def plot_words(word_counts, n=10):
    """Plot a bar chart of word counts.

    Parameters
    ----------
    word_counts : collections.Counter
        Counter object of word counts.
    n : int, optional
        Plot the top n words. By default, 10.
```

```
...rest of docstring hidden...
"""
top_n_words = word_counts.most_common(n)
word, count = zip(*top_n_words)
fig = plt.bar(range(n), count)
plt.xticks(range(n), labels=word, rotation=45)
plt.xlabel("Word")
plt.ylabel("Count")
return fig
```

Our function takes in a `Counter` object of word counts and outputs a `mat-plotlib` bar chart. To test that it's working as expected with a unit test, we'll:

- Use the manually counted words from the Einstein quote as a fixture.
- Use that fixture as an input to the `plot_words()` function to create a bar plot (the actual result).
- `assert` that the plot is a `matplotlib` bar chart (`matplotlib.container.BarContainer`) and `assert` that there are ten bars in the bar chart (`n=10` is the default number of bars to plot in the `plot_words()` function, as you can see above).

Below we show this unit test in Python code, and we'll add it to our *test_pycounts.py* file:

```
from pycounts.pycounts import count_words
from pycounts.plotting import plot_words    <---------
import matplotlib                           <---------
from collections import Counter

def test_count_words():
    # ... same as before ...

def test_plot_words():    <---------
    """Test plotting of word counts."""
    counts = Counter({'insanity': 1, 'is': 1, 'doing': 1,
                      'the': 1, 'same': 1, 'thing': 1,
                      'over': 2, 'and': 2, 'expecting': 1,
                      'different': 1, 'results': 1})
    fig = plot_words(counts)
    assert isinstance(fig, matplotlib.container.BarContainer), \
        "Wrong plot type"
    assert len(fig.datavalues) == 10, \
        "Incorrect number of bars plotted"
```

Now that we've written a new test, we need to check that it is working. Running `pytest` at the command line should now show two tests were run:

```
$ pytest tests/
```

```
========================= test session starts =========================
...
collected 2 item

tests/test_pycounts.py .                                        [100%]

========================= 2 passed in 0.01s =========================
```

Looks like things are working as expected!

Before we move on, there's one more important thing to mention. We know that the `assert` statement can be used with any expression that evaluates to a boolean (`True`/`False`). However, if your package uses floating-point numbers, and you're wanting to `assert` the equality of floating-point numbers in your tests, there's one thing to watch out for. Due to the limitations of floating-point arithmetic in computers, numbers that we would expect to be equal are sometimes not. Consider the following infamous example:

```
>>> assert 0.1 + 0.2 == 0.3, "Numbers are not equal!"
```

```
AssertionError: Numbers are not equal!
```

You can read more about the nuances of floating-point arithmetic in the Python documentation[2], but the important point here is that, when working with floating-point numbers, we usually `assert` that numbers are *approximately* equal, rather than *exactly* equal. To do this we can use the `pytest.approx()` function:

```
>>> import pytest
>>> assert 0.1 + 0.2 == pytest.approx(0.3), "Numbers are not equal!"
```

You can control how approximate you want the equality to be by using the abs and `rel` arguments of `pytest.approx()` to specify how much absolute or relative error you want to allow, respectively.

---

[2]`https://docs.python.org/3/tutorial/floatingpoint.html`

5.3.2   Test that a specific error is raised

Rather than `assert` that your code produces a particular output given a particular input, sometimes you want to check that your code raises a particular error when used in the wrong way by a user. Consider again the `plot_words()` function of our `pycounts.plotting` module. From the docstring, we see that the function expects users to pass a `Counter` object to the function:

```python
import matplotlib.pyplot as plt

def plot_words(word_counts, n=10):
    """Plot a bar chart of word counts.

    Parameters
    ----------
    word_counts : collections.Counter   <--------
        Counter object of word counts.
    n : int, optional
        Plot the top n words. By default, 10.

    ...rest of docstring hidden...
    """
    top_n_words = word_counts.most_common(n)
    word, count = zip(*top_n_words)
    fig = plt.bar(range(n), count)
    plt.xticks(range(n), labels=word, rotation=45)
    plt.xlabel("Word")
    plt.ylabel("Count")
    return fig
```

What happens if a user inputs a different object? For the sake of argument, let's consider what happens if they pass a list of words to our function:

```python
>>> from pycounts.plotting import plot_words
>>> word_list = ["Pythons", "are", "non", "venomous"]
>>> plot_words(word_list)
```

```
AttributeError: 'list' object has no attribute 'most_common'
```

This `AttributeError` message is not overly useful to our users. The problem is that our code uses the method `.most_common()`, which is specific to the `Counter` object and retrieves the top n counts from that object. To improve the user-experience, we might want to raise a more helpful error message to a user to tell them if they pass the wrong object type.

Let's modify our `plot_words()` function to check that the `word_counts` argument is a `Counter` object using the `isinstance()` function and, if it's not, raise a `TypeError` with a useful message. The `raise` statement terminates a program and allows you to notify users of an error. There are many error types to choose from and you can even create your own, as discussed in the Python documentation[3]. We'll use the `TypeError` here because it is used to indicate that an object is of the wrong type. Our function, with this new checking code in it, now looks like this:

```
import matplotlib.pyplot as plt
from collections import Counter   <--------

def plot_words(word_counts, n=10):
    """Plot a bar chart of word counts.

    ...rest of docstring hidden...
    """
    if not isinstance(word_counts, Counter):   <--------
        raise TypeError("'word_counts' should be of type 'Counter'.")
    top_n_words = word_counts.most_common(n)
    word, count = zip(*top_n_words)
    fig = plt.bar(range(n), count)
    plt.xticks(range(n), labels=word, rotation=45)
    plt.xlabel("Word")
    plt.ylabel("Count")
    return fig
```

Other commons exceptions used in tests include:

- `AttributeError`: for when an object does not support a referenced attribute (i.e., of the form `object.attribute`).
- `ValueError`: for when an argument has the right type but an inappropriate value.
- `FileNotFoundError`: for when a specified file or directory doesn't exist.
- `ImportError`: for when the `import` statement can't find a module.

We can check that our new error-handling code is working by starting a new

---

[3]`https://docs.python.org/3/library/exceptions.html`

Python session and retrying our code from before, which passed a `list` to our function:

```
>>> from pycounts.plotting import plot_words
>>> word_list = ["Pythons", "are", "non", "venomous"]
>>> plot_words(word_list)


TypeError: 'word_counts' should be of type 'Counter'.
```

Great, our `plot_words()` function now raises a helpful `TypeError` when a user inputs the wrong type of object. But how can we test this functionality with `pytest`? We can use `pytest.raises()`. `pytest.raises()` is used as part of a `with` statement, which contains the code you expect to throw an error. Let's add the new unit test shown below, called `test_plot_words_error()`, to our test file `test_pycounts.py` to demonstrate this functionality.

We've written a new test called `test_plot_words_error()`, rather than adding to our existing `test_plot_words()` test, because unit tests should be written to check one unit of code (i.e., a function) in one particular situation.

```
from pycounts.pycounts import count_words
from pycounts.plotting import plot_words
import matplotlib
from collections import Counter
import pytest   <--------

def test_count_words():
    # ... same as before ...

def test_plot_words():
    # ... same as before ...

def test_plot_words_error():   <--------
    """Check TypeError raised when Counter not used."""
    with pytest.raises(TypeError):
        list_object = ["Pythons", "are", "non", "venomous"]
        plot_words(list_object)
```

In the new test above, we purposefully pass the wrong object type (a list) to `plot_words()` and expect it to raise a `TypeError`. Let's check that this new test, and our existing tests, all pass by running `pytest` at the terminal. `pytest` should now find and execute three tests:

```
$ pytest tests/
```

```
========================= test session starts =========================
...
collected 3 items

tests/test_pycounts.py .                                    [100%]

========================= 3 passed in 0.39s =========================
```

5.3.3 Integration tests

The unit tests we've written above verify that the individual functions of our package work in isolation. But we should also test that they work correctly together. Such a test is called an "integration test" (because individual units of code are integrated into a single test).

Integration tests are structured the same way as unit tests. We use a fixture to produce an actual result with our code, which is then compared to an expected result. As an example of an integration test we'll:

- Use the "Einstein quote" text file, *einstein.txt*, as a fixture.
- Count the words in the quote using the `count_words()` function.
- Plot the word counts using the `plot_words()` function.
- `assert` that a `matplotlib` bar chart was created, that the chart has 10 bars, and that the maximum word count in the chart is 2 (no word appears more than twice in the quote in the *einstein.txt* file).

The overall aim of this test is to check that the two core functions of our package `count_words()` and `plot_words()` work together (at least to our test specifications). It can be written and added to our *test_pycounts.py* file as follows:

```python
from pycounts.pycounts import count_words
from pycounts.plotting import plot_words
import matplotlib
from collections import Counter
import pytest
```

```
def test_count_words():
    # ... same as before ...

def test_plot_words():
    # ... same as before ...

def test_plot_words_error():
    # ... same as before ...

def test_integration():  <--------
    """Test count_words() and plot_words() workflow."""
    counts = count_words("tests/einstein.txt")
    fig = plot_words(counts)
    assert isinstance(fig, matplotlib.container.BarContainer), \
        "Wrong plot type"
    assert len(fig.datavalues) == 10, \
        "Incorrect number of bars plotted"
    assert max(fig.datavalues) == 2, "Highest word count should be 2"
```

pytest should now find and execute four tests:

```
$ pytest tests/
```

```
=========================== test session starts ===========================
...
collected 4 items

tests/test_pycounts.py .                                          [100%]

============================ 4 passed in 0.39s ============================
```

5.3.4 Regression tests

We've been testing our pycounts package on the simple "Einstein quote" fixture, but how does it perform on real data? We added some example real data to our package in **Section 4.2.6**; a *.txt* file of the novel *Flatland*, by Edwin Abbott (Abbott, 1884) (available online[4]). However, it would be impossible to count all of the words in that text by hand to come up with an "expected" result.

---

[4]https://www.gutenberg.org/ebooks/97

Instead, regression testing is about testing that your code produces consistent results as opposed to expected results. The idea is to see how our package performs on this data now, and add a test to check that the result stays consistent in the future as we add more functionality to our package.

For example, the most-common words in *Flatland* can be determined as follows:

```
>>> from pycounts.datasets import get_flatland
>>> from pycounts.pycounts import count_words
>>> counts = count_words(get_flatland())
>>> counts.most_common(1)
```

```
[('the', 2244)]
```

Unsurprisingly, the most common word is "the" which occurs 2245 times. An example regression test for our package would, therefore, look as follows:

```
from pycounts.pycounts import count_words
from pycounts.plotting import plot_words
from pycounts.datasets import get_flatland    <--------
import matplotlib
from collections import Counter
import pytest


def test_count_words():
    # ... same as before ...


def test_plot_words():
    # ... same as before ...


def test_plot_words_error():
    # ... same as before ...


def test_integration():
    # ... same as before ...


def test_regression():    <--------
    """Regression test for Flatland"""
    top_word = count_words(get_flatland()).most_common(1)
    assert top_word[0][0] == "the", "Most common word is not 'the'"
    assert top_word[0][1] == 2244, "'the' count has changed"
```

pytest should now find and execute five tests:

```
$ pytest tests/
```

```
========================== test session starts ==========================
...
collected 5 items

tests/test_pycounts.py .                                          [100%]

========================== 5 passed in 0.39s ==========================
```

5.3.5   How many tests should you write

Now that you know how to write tests, how many should you actually write?
There's no single answer to this question. In general, you want your tests to
evaluate the core functionality of your program. Code coverage, which we'll
discuss in **Section 3.7.3**, is a metric that can help you understand how much
of your code your tests actually evaluate. But even 100% coverage doesn't
guarantee your code is perfect, only that it passes the specific tests you wrote!

It might be near impossible to write tests for every single use-case of your
package (you'd be amazed at the weird and wonderful ways users can find to
unwittingly break your code!). That's why testing is an iterative procedure,
as we discussed in **Section 5.1**; as you refactor and add to your code, as users
find ways to use your function that you didn't expect, or it produces results
you didn't account for, write new tests, write new code, run your tests, and
repeat.

5.4   Advanced testing methods

As the complexity and number of tests you write increases, it can be helpful to
streamline and organize your tests in a more efficient and accessible manner.
pytest fixtures and parameterizations are two useful concepts that can help
here. As we'll next discuss, pytest fixtures can be used to more efficiently
define the context for your tests (e.g., the data or directory structure they run
in), and parameterizations allow you to run the same test multiple times but
with different input and output values.

5.4.1 Fixtures

Our current `test_pycounts.py` file contains the same fixture defined multiple times; a `Counter` object of the words in the "Einstein quote".

```python
from pycounts.pycounts import count_words
from pycounts.plotting import plot_words
from pycounts.datasets import get_flatland
import matplotlib
from collections import Counter
import pytest

def test_count_words():
    """Test word counting from a file."""
    expected = Counter({'insanity': 1, 'is': 1, 'doing': 1,
                        'the': 1, 'same': 1, 'thing': 1,
                        'over': 2, 'and': 2, 'expecting': 1,
                        'different': 1, 'results': 1})
    actual = count_words("tests/einstein.txt")
    assert actual == expected, "Einstein quote counted incorrectly!"

def test_plot_words():
    """Test plotting of word counts."""
    counts = Counter({'insanity': 1, 'is': 1, 'doing': 1,
                      'the': 1, 'same': 1, 'thing': 1,
                      'over': 2, 'and': 2, 'expecting': 1,
                      'different': 1, 'results': 1})
    fig = plot_words(counts)
    assert isinstance(fig, matplotlib.container.BarContainer), \
        "Wrong plot type"
    assert len(fig.datavalues) == 10, "Incorrect number of bars plotted"

... rest of file hidden ...
```

This is inefficient and violates the "don't repeat yourself" (DRY) principle of software development. Fortunately, there's a solution. In `pytest`, fixtures can be defined as functions that can be reused across your test suite. In our case, we could create a fixture that defines the "Einstein quote" `Counter` object, and makes it available to any test that wants to use it.

It's easiest to see the utility of a fixture by example. Fixtures can be created in `pytest` using the `@pytest.fixture` decorator. A decorator in Python is defined using the @ symbol and immediately precedes a function definition. Decorators add functionality to the function they are "decorating"; understanding them isn't necessary to use them here, but for those interested in learning more, check out this Primer on Python Decorators[5].

In the code below, we define a function called `einstein_counts()` and decorate it with the `@pytest.fixture` decorator. This fixture returns the manually counted words in the Einstein quote as a `Counter` object. To use it in a test, we pass it as an parameter to the test function, just like you would usually specify a function parameter, e.g., `test_count_words(einstein_counts)`. We'll use our new fixture in both the `test_count_words()` and `test_plot_words()` below:

```python
from pycounts.pycounts import count_words
from pycounts.plotting import plot_words
from pycounts.datasets import get_flatland
import matplotlib
from collections import Counter
import pytest

@pytest.fixture              <--------
def einstein_counts():   <--------
    return Counter({'insanity': 1, 'is': 1, 'doing': 1,
                    'the': 1, 'same': 1, 'thing': 1,
                    'over': 2, 'and': 2, 'expecting': 1,
                    'different': 1, 'results': 1})

def test_count_words(einstein_counts):   <--------
    """Test word counting from a file."""
    expected = einstein_counts
    actual = count_words("tests/einstein.txt")
    assert actual == expected, "Einstein quote counted incorrectly!"

def test_plot_words(einstein_counts):   <--------
    """Test plotting of word counts."""
    fig = plot_words(einstein_counts)
    assert isinstance(fig, matplotlib.container.BarContainer), \
        "Wrong plot type"
    assert len(fig.datavalues) == 10, "Incorrect number of bars plotted"

... rest of file hidden ...
```

We now have a way of defining a fixture once but using it in multiple tests.

At this point you might wonder why we used the `@pytest.fixture` decorator

---

[5]https://realpython.com/primer-on-python-decorators

at all, why not just define a variable as normal at the top of the script like this:

```
from pycounts.pycounts import count_words
from pycounts.plotting import plot_words
from pycounts.datasets import get_flatland
import matplotlib
from collections import Counter
import pytest


einstein_counts = Counter({'insanity': 1, 'is': 1, 'doing': 1,
                           'the': 1, 'same': 1, 'thing': 1,
                           'over': 2, 'and': 2, 'expecting': 1,
                           'different': 1, 'results': 1})

def test_count_words():
    """Test word counting from a file."""
    expected = einstein_counts

# ... rest of file hidden ...
```

The short answer is that fixtures provide far more functionality and reliability than manually defined variables. For example, each time you use a pytest fixture, it triggers the fixture function, meaning that each test gets a fresh copy of the data; you don't have to worry about accidentally mutating or deleting your fixture during a test session. You can also control this behavior; should the fixture be executed once per use, once per test module, or once per test session? This can be helpful if the fixture is large or time-consuming to create. Finally, we've only explored the use of fixtures as data for a test, but fixtures can also be used to set up the environment for a test. For example, the directory structure a test should run in, or the environment variables it should have access to. pytest fixtures can help you easily set up these kinds of contexts, as you can read more about in the pytest documentation[6].

5.4.2 Parameterizations

Parameterizations can be useful for running a test multiple times using different arguments. For example, recall in **Section 5.3.2** that we added some code to pycounts's plot_words() function that raises a TypeError if a user inputs an object other than a Counter object to the function. We wrote a test to check that in our *test_pycounts.py* file as follows:

---

[6]https://pytest.readthedocs.io/en/latest/fixture.html

```
# ... rest of file hidden ...

def test_plot_words_error():
    """Check TypeError raised when Counter not used."""
    with pytest.raises(TypeError):
        list_object = ["Pythons", "are", "non", "venomous"]
        plot_words(list_object)

# ... rest of file hidden ...
```

Our test only tests the `TypeError` is raised if a `list` object is passed as an input, but we should also test what happens if other objects are passed too, such as numbers or strings. Rather than writing new tests for each object we want to try, we can parameterize this test with all the different data we want to try, and pytest will run the test for each piece of data.

Parameterizations can be created in pytest using the `@pytest.mark.parametrize(argnames, argvalues)` decorator. `argnames` represent the names of test variable(s) you want to use in your test function (you can use any name you want), and `argvalues` is a list of the values those test variable(s) will take.

In the code example below, that we've added to the `test_pycounts.py` file, we create a test variable named `obj`, which can take three values; a float (`3.141`), a string (`"test.txt"`), or a list of strings (`["list", "of", "words"]`). With this parameterization, pytest will run our test three times, once for each value that we specified we want `obj` to take.

```
# ... rest of file hidden ...

@pytest.mark.parametrize(
    "obj",
    [
        3.141,
        "test.txt",
        ["list", "of", "words"]
    ]
)
def test_plot_words_error(obj):
    """Check TypeError raised when Counter not used."""
    with pytest.raises(TypeError):
        plot_words(obj)

# ... rest of file hidden ...
```

We can explicitly show that `pytest` will run our test three times (once for each value we specified) by adding the `--verbose` flag to our `pytest` command:

```
$ pytest tests/ --verbose
```

```
========================= test session starts =========================
...
collected 7 items

tests/test_pycounts.py::test_count_words PASSED                [ 14%]
tests/test_pycounts.py::test_plot_words PASSED                 [ 28%]
tests/test_pycounts.py::test_plot_words_error[3.141] PASSED    [ 42%]
tests/test_pycounts.py::test_plot_words_error[test.txt] PASSED [ 57%]
tests/test_pycounts.py::test_plot_words_error[obj2] PASSED     [ 71%]
tests/test_pycounts.py::test_integration PASSED                [ 85%]
tests/test_pycounts.py::test_regression PASSED                 [100%]

========================= 7 passed in 0.52s =========================
```

Sometimes you'll want to run a test on a function, where the output depends on the input. As an example, consider the function `is_even()` below:

```
def is_even(n):
    """Check if n is even."""
    if n % 2 == 0:
        return True
    else:
        return False
```

To parameterize this test with different input/output pairs, we use the same syntax as before with `@pytest.mark.parametrize()` except we comma-separate the test arguments in a string (`"n, result"`) and group the pairs of values we want those arguments to take in a tuple (e.g., `(2, True)`, `(3, False)`, etc.). In the example test that follows, we'll purposefully add a wrong input/output pair (`(4, False)`) to show what the output of `pytest` looks like in the case of a failed parameterization:

```
@pytest.mark.parametrize(
    "n, result",
    [
        (2, True),
        (3, False),
        (4, False)  # this last pair is purposefully wrong so we can
```

```
                        # show an example of the pytest error message
    ]
)
def test_is_even(n, result):
    assert is_even(n) == result
```

The above test would run successfully for the first two parameterized in-
put/output pairs but would fail for the last one with the following helpful
error message that points out exactly which parameterization failed:

```
---
emphasize-lines: 4, 19
---
============================== FAILURES ==============================
_____ testis_even[4-False] _____

n = 4, result = False

    @pytest.mark.parametrize(
        "n, result",
        [
            (2, True),
            (3, False),
            (4, False)
        ]
    )
    def testis_even(n, result):
>       assert is_even(n) == result

tests/test_example.py:13: AssertionError
======================= short test summary info =======================
FAILED tests/test_example.py:testis_even[4-False]: assert True == False
```

You can read more about parameterizations in the pytest documentation[7].

5.5   Code coverage

A good test suite will contain tests that check as much of your package's code
as possible. How much of your code your tests actually use is called "code

---

[7] https://docs.pytest.org/en/6.2.x/parametrize.html

coverage", and there are different ways to calculate it, as we'll learn about in this section.

5.5.1 Line coverage

The simplest and most intuitive measure of code coverage is line coverage. It is the proportion of lines of your package's code that are executed by your tests:

$$\text{coverage} = \frac{\text{lines executed}}{\text{total lines}} * 100\%$$

Consider the following hypothetical code, consisting of 9 lines:

```python
def myfunc(x):                      # Line 1
    if x > 0:                       # Line 2
        print("x above threshold!") # Line 3
        print("Running analysis.")  # Line 4
        y = round(x)                # Line 5
        z = y ** 2                  # Line 6
    elif x < 0:                     # Line 7
        z = abs(x)                  # Line 8
    return z                        # Line 9
```

Imagine we write the following unit test for that code. This unit test uses x=10.25 as a test fixture (if you follow the code above, you'll see that the expected result for that fixture is 100):

```python
def test_myfunc_1():
    assert myfunc(x=10.25) == 100
```

This test only covers the condition x > 0 of our myfunc() function and hence will only execute lines 1 — 6 and line 9; a total of 7, of 9, possible lines. The coverage would therefore be:

$$\text{coverage} = \frac{7}{9} * 100\% = 78\%$$

Line coverage is simple and intuitive to understand, and many developers use it as a measure of how much of their package's code is covered by their tests. But you can see how line coverage can potentially be misleading. Our myfunc() function has two possible outputs, depending on which condition of the if statement is satisfied. These two possible code paths are called "branches", and they might be equally important to our package, but our line coverage metric is heavily dependent on which branches we actually test. Imagine if we used the test below for our myfunc() function, which passes a value x <= 0:

```
def test_myfunc_2():
    assert myfunc(x=-5) == 5
```

This test only covers line 1, 2 and lines 7-9 of the function, for a total of 5 lines and 56% coverage. Because line coverage can be skewed (or artificially inflated) by how many lines are in the branches of your code, some developers prefer to calculate branch coverage, which we'll talk about in the next section.

5.5.2   Branch coverage

In contrast to line coverage, branch coverage evaluates how many branches in your code are executed by tests, where a branch is a possible execution path the code can take, usually in the form of an `if` statement.

```
def myfunc(x):
    # Branch 1
    if x > 0:
        print("x above threshold!")
        print("Running analysis.")
        y = round(x)
        z = y ** 2
    # Branch 2
    elif x < 0:
        z = abs(x)
    return z
```

$$\text{coverage} = \frac{\text{branches executed}}{\text{total branches}} * 100\%$$

When using branch coverage, we would get 50% coverage regardless of whether we ran the `test_myfunc_1()` or `test_myfunc_2()` test functions we defined in **Section 5.5.1** because each test covers one branch. While line coverage is perhaps more intuitive and easier to understand than branch coverage, many developers feel that branch coverage provides a more useful, less-biased, measure of coverage. In the next section, we'll show how to calculate coverage as a mix of line and branch coverage, to get the best of both metrics.

5.5.3   Calculating coverage

We can calculate code coverage with `pytest` using the extension `pytest-cov`. For a `poetry`-managed package, `pytest-cov` can be installed as a development dependency with the following command:

```
$ poetry add --dev pytest-cov
```

---

pytest-cov is an implementation of the coverage package. It can sometimes be helpful to visit the latter's documentation[8] if you're looking for more information about how pytest-cov calculates coverage.

Code coverage can be calculated using the pytest command with the argument --cov=<pkg-name> specified. For example, the following command determines the coverage our tests have of our pycounts package:

```
$ pytest tests/ --cov=pycounts
```

```
========================= test session starts =========================

Name                            Stmts   Miss  Cover
-----------------------------------------------------
src/pycounts/__init__.py            2      0   100%
src/pycounts/data/__init__.py       0      0   100%
src/pycounts/datasets.py            5      0   100%
src/pycounts/plotting.py           12      0   100%
src/pycounts/pycounts.py           16      0   100%
-----------------------------------------------------
TOTAL                              35      0   100%

========================= 7 passed in 0.46s =========================
```

The output summarizes the coverage of the individual modules in our pycounts package. By default, pytest-cov calculates coverage as line coverage. Stmts is how many lines are in a module, Miss is how many lines were not executed by tests, and Cover is the percentage of lines executed by your tests. After having made our way through this chapter, we've written enough tests to obtain 100 percent line coverage for our pycounts modules! But note that 100 percent coverage doesn't guarantee our code is perfect, only that it passes the specific tests we wrote!

---

[8]https://coverage.readthedocs.io/en/latest/

If we want to calculate branch coverage with `pytest`, we can specify the argument `--cov-branch`:

```
$ pytest --cov=pycounts --cov-branch
```

```
========================= test session starts =========================

Name                              Stmts   Miss Branch BrPart  Cover
-----------------------------------------------------------------------
src/pycounts/__init__.py              2      0      0      0   100%
src/pycounts/data/__init__.py         0      0      0      0   100%
src/pycounts/datasets.py              5      0      0      0   100%
src/pycounts/plotting.py             12      0      2      0   100%
src/pycounts/pycounts.py             16      0      2      0   100%
-----------------------------------------------------------------------
TOTAL                                35      0      4      0   100%

========================= 5 passed in 0.46s =========================
```

In this output `Branch` is the number of branches in the module, and `BrPart` is the number of branches executed by tests. "Branch coverage" in `pytest-cov` is actually calculated using a mix of branch and line coverage, which can be useful to get the best of both metrics:

$$\text{coverage} = \frac{\text{lines executed} + \text{branches executed}}{\text{total lines} + \text{total branches}} * 100\%$$

5.5.4   Coverage reports

As we've seen, `pytest --cov` provides a helpful high-level summary of our test coverage at the command line. But if we want to see a more detailed output we can generate a useful HTML report using the argument `--cov-report html` as follows:

```
$ pytest --cov=pycounts --cov-report html
```

The report will be available at *htmlcov/index.html* (relative to your working directory) and will look like Fig. 5.2.

We can click on elements of the report, like the *datasets.py* module, to see exactly what lines/branches the tests are hitting/missing, as shown in Fig. 5.3:

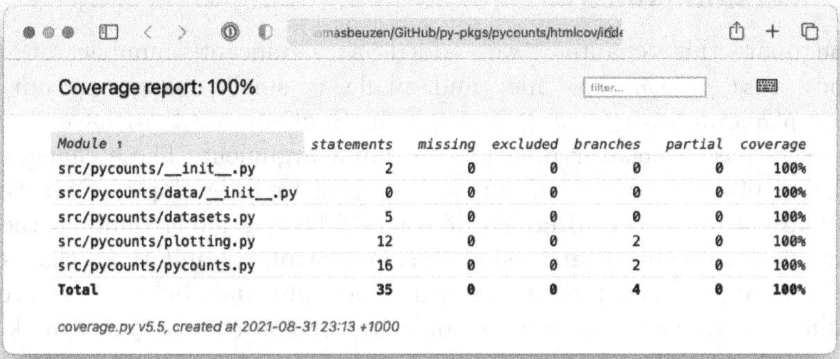

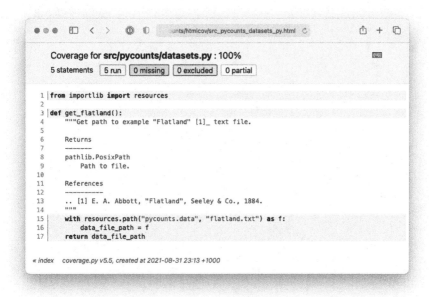

FIGURE 5.2: HTML test report.

FIGURE 5.3: Detailed view of the datasets module in the HTML report.

5.6 Version control

Throughout this chapter, we added a significant number of tests to our *test_pycounts.py* file, and made a small change to our py-counts.plotting.plot_words() function in **Section 5.3.2** to have it check that users pass a Counter object as an input argument. These changes will form part of a new release of our package that we'll develop in **Chapter 7: Releasing and versioning**. So, if you're following along building the py-counts package yourself and using version control, commit these changes to your local and remote repositories using the commands below. If you're not building the pycounts package or not using version control, you can skip to the next chapter.

```
$ git add tests/test_pycounts.py
$ git commit -m "test: add additional tests for all modules"
$ git add src/pycounts/plotting.py
$ git commit -m "fix: check input type to plot_words function"
$ git push
```

6

Documentation

Writing documentation for your package is arguably one of the most important, but perhaps least exciting, parts of the packaging process. The purpose of documentation is to help users understand how they can use and interact with your package, without having to read the source code. For the users of your code (including your future self), having readable and accessible documentation is invaluable. The reality is, if no one knows how to use your package, it will probably not get used!

In **Section 3.8**, we walked through the steps required to create documentation, compile it into a user-friendly and shareable HTML format, and then host it online. We'll revise those steps here and will provide more detail about the documentation workflow and the individual elements of package documentation.

6.1 Documentation content and workflow

To give you an idea of what we mean when we say "documentation", Table 6.1 shows the documentation included with a typical Python package and where it is usually located in the package's directory structure.

TABLE 6.1: Typical Python package documentation.

Documentation	Typical location	Description
README	Root	Provides high-level information about the package, e.g., what it does, how to install it, and how to use it.
License	Root	Explains who owns the copyright to your package source and how it can be used and shared.

Documentation	Typical location	Description
Contributing guidelines	Root	Explains how to contribute to the project.
Code of conduct	Root	Defines standards for how to appropriately engage with and contribute to the project and its community.
Changelog	Root	A chronologically ordered list of notable changes to the package over time, usually organized by version.
Docstrings	*.py* files	Text appearing as the first statement in a function, method, class, or module in Python that describes what the code does and how to use it. Accessible to users via the `help()` command.
Examples	*docs/*	Step-by-step, tutorial-like examples showing how the package works in more detail.
API reference	*docs/*	An organized list of the user-facing functionality of your package (i.e., functions, classes, etc.) along with a short description of what they do and how to use them. Typically created automatically from your package's docstrings using the `sphinx` tool as we'll discuss in **Section 3.8.4**.

We'll discuss what each of these pieces of documentation are and how to write them in **Section 3.8.1**. But it's first helpful to understand the big-picture documentation workflow and what we're aiming to build.

The typical workflow for documenting a Python package consists of three steps:

1. **Write documentation**: manually write the documentation source files that will support your package, such as those listed in Table 6.1. These are usually written in a plain-text format like Markdown[1] (*.md*). reStructuredText[2] (*.rst*), which we explain in **Section 3.8.1**. Below we show an example of the *README.md* file we wrote for the pycounts package we developed in **Chapter 3: How to package a Python.**

```
# pycounts

Calculate word counts in a text file!

## Installation

```bash
$ pip install pycounts
```

Usage

`pycounts` can be used to count words in a text file and plot
results as follows:

```python
from pycounts.pycounts import count_words
from pycounts.plotting import plot_words
import matplotlib.pyplot as plt

file_path = "test.txt"  # path to your file
counts = count_words(file_path)
fig = plot_words(counts, n=10)
plt.show()
```

    ...rest of file hidden...
```

---

[1]https://en.wikipedia.org/wiki/Markdown
[2]https://www.sphinx-doc.org/en/master/usage/restructuredtext/index.html

2. **Build documentation**: compile and render the manually written documentation into an organized, coherent, and shareable format, such as HTML or PDF, using the documentation generator tool sphinx. To help you understand what this means, Fig. 6.1 shows an example of what the README document above looks like when it's "built".

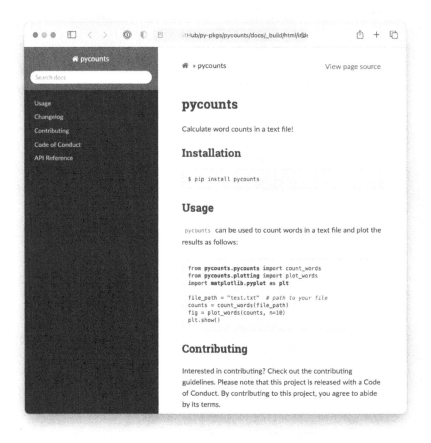

FIGURE 6.1: Example of HTML documentation generated by sphinx.

3. **Host documentation online**: share documentation online so it can be easily accessed by anyone with an internet connection, using a free service like Read the Docs[3] or GitHub Pages[4]. For example, the documentation we built for pycounts in **Section 3.8** is available online at https://pycounts.readthedocs.io/en/latest/.

---

[3]https://readthedocs.org
[4]https://pages.github.com

In the remaining sections of this chapter, we'll walk through each of the above steps of the documentation workflow.

6.2 Writing documentation

Table 6.1 shows the typical documentation included in a package and where it is usually located in the package's directory structure. There's a lot of content to think about here, but the reality is that most developers make Python packages from templates that create most of this documentation automatically. For example, consider the `pycounts` package we created using the `py-pkgs-cookiecutter` template in **Section 3.2.2**:

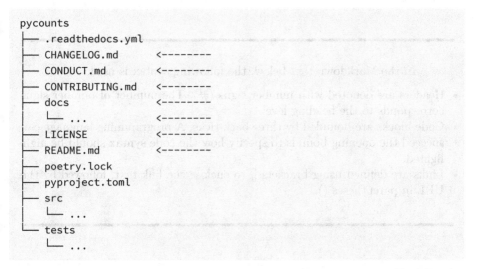

```
pycounts
├── .readthedocs.yml
├── CHANGELOG.md        <--------
├── CONDUCT.md          <--------
├── CONTRIBUTING.md     <--------
├── docs                <--------
│   └── ...             <--------
├── LICENSE             <--------
├── README.md           <--------
├── poetry.lock
├── pyproject.toml
├── src
│   └── ...
└── tests
    └── ...
```

Documentation is typically written in a plain-text markup format, such as Markdown[5] (*.md*) or reStructuredText[6] (*.rst*). With a plain-text markup language, documents are written in plain-text and a special syntax is used to specify how the text should be formatted when it is rendered by a suitable tool. We saw an example of a raw and rendered Markdown document in **Section 6.1**. As you can see from the structure of our `pycounts` package above, we use Markdown (*.md*) in this book because it is widely used, and we feel it has a less verbose and more intuitive syntax than reStructuredText. Automatic Markdown-rendering is also supported on a wide variety of IDEs and websites. We'll show examples of Markdown syntax and writing the documents above in

---

[5]https://en.wikipedia.org/wiki/Markdown
[6]https://www.sphinx-doc.org/en/master/usage/restructuredtext/index.html

the following sections, and you can check out the Markdown Guide[7] to learn more about Markdown.

6.2.1   README

The README file is the "map" of your package. It's typically the first thing users will see and read when interacting with your package and should provide high-level information such as: what your package does, how it can be installed, a brief demonstration of usage, who created the package, how it is licensed, and how to contribute to it. The README is the "gateway" to your package. Without it, users won't know where to begin.

As an example of a README file, we show the full README of our `pycounts` package below, which we developed in **Chapter 3: How to package a Python.**

In the Markdown text below, the following syntax is used:

- Headers are denoted with number signs (#). The number of number signs corresponds to the heading level.
- Code blocks are bounded by three back-ticks. A programming language can succeed the opening bounds to specify how the code syntax should be highlighted.
- Links are defined using brackets [] to enclose the link text, followed by the URL in parentheses ().

```
# pycounts

Calculate word counts in a text file!

## Installation

```bash
$ pip install pycounts
```

Usage
```

`pycounts` can be used to count words in a text file and plot results
as follows:

````python
```python
from pycounts.pycounts import count_words
from pycounts.plotting import plot_words
import matplotlib.pyplot as plt

file_path = "test.txt"  # path to your file
counts = count_words(file_path)
fig = plot_words(counts, n=10)
plt.show()
```
````

Contributing

Interested in contributing? Check out the contributing guidelines.
Please note that this project is released with a Code of Conduct.
By contributing to this project, you agree to abide by its terms.

License

`pycounts` was created by Tomas Beuzen. It is licensed under the terms
of the MIT license.

Credits

`pycounts` was created with
[`cookiecutter`](https://cookiecutter.readthedocs.io/en/latest/) and
the `py-pkgs-cookiecutter`
[template](https://github.com/py-pkgs/py-pkgs-cookiecutter).

To stress the point once more, while the raw text above doesn't look like much,
the Markdown syntax formats the text nicely when rendered by a tool like
sphinx into what we showed in Fig. 6.1. This is why we use Markdown to write
package documentation — it can be easily written in plain-text but renders
into something so much more!

6.2.2   License

A license tells others what they can and can't do with your code. The Open
Source Initiative (OSI)[8] is a good place to learn more about different licenses,

---

[8]https://opensource.org/

and GitHub also has a useful tool[9] for helping choose the most appropriate license for your package. Some common licenses used for Python packages include:

- Creative Commons CC0 1.0 Universal (CC0 1.0): releases your software into the public domain, such that others can use it for any purpose.
- MIT license: allows users to do whatever they want with your software, as long as they include the original copyright and license notice in any copy or substantial modification of it.
- GNU General Public License v3 (GPL-3): less permissive than the above licenses. Any changes made to your software must be recorded, and the complete source code of the original software and modifications of it must be made available under the same GPL-3 license.

If you don't include a license, then default copyright laws apply, which typically means that you retain all rights to your source code, and no one may download, reproduce, distribute, or create derivative works from your package. This might be fine if you want to keep your work private or proprietary, but if you open-source your work without a license, others will be unable to use or contribute to it.

6.2.3   Contributing guidelines

A contributing guidelines file (often named "CONTRIBUTING") outlines procedures for how users can contribute to your project. These guidelines will vary depending on how you're sharing your package's source with others, but they typically include information on what kinds of contributions you're accepting, and how to make those contributions (usually via the use of a version control system). GitHub provides a good guide[10] for adding a contributing file to your project.

Having clear contributing guidelines streamlines the incorporation of contributions into your package. Without contributing guidelines, it's not clear how others should effectively contribute, or if you would like contributions at all. As a result, you may receive contributions you don't want, or in a way you don't want, which could waste your and other people's time.

6.2.4   Code of conduct

A code of conduct file (often named "CONDUCT") is used to define community standards, identify a welcoming and inclusive project, and outline

---

[9]https://choosealicense.com/

[10]https://help.github.com/en/github/building-a-strong-community/setting-guidelines-for-repository-contributors

procedures for handling abuse. GitHub provides an excellent guide[11] for adding a code of conduct to your project. A code of conduct helps the community feel safe, respected, and welcome to contribute to your package. Without it, others may not want to contribute to your package, and conflicts may arise among contributors with conflicting ideas.

6.2.5 Changelog

A changelog is a file which contains a chronologically ordered list of changes made to your package. Changes are typically organized per released version of your package, something we'll discuss more in **Chapter 7: Releasing and versioning**. Having a changelog helps users and contributors understand the history of a package and how it has evolved over time. Without it, there's no easy way for users to understand when, what, and why changes were made to your package.

Changelog's are made for humans to read. They typically contain dot-points of important changes made for each version of your package, grouped into categories such as: "Feature", "Fix", "Documentation", "Tests", and with the latest version at the top of the file. An example of a hypothetical changelog for our `pycounts` package is shown below.

In the Markdown text below the syntax `<!-- ... -->` indicates a comment. Comments aren't included in the rendered version of the document.

```
# Changelog

<!--next-version-placeholder-->

## v0.2.1 (12/09/2021)

### Fix

- Changed confusing error message in plotting.plot_words()

## v0.2.0 (10/09/2021)
```

---

[11]https://help.github.com/en/github/building-a-strong-community/adding-a-code-of-conduct-to-your-project

```
### Feature

- Added a "stop_words" argument to pycounts.count_words()

### Documentation

- Added new usage examples
- Now hosting documentation on Read the Docs

## v0.1.0 (24/08/2021)

- First release of `pycounts`
```

In **Chapter 8: Continuous integration and deployment,** we'll show how you can automatically update your changelog from your version control commit messages when you make a new release of your package.

6.2.6 Examples

Creating examples of how to use your package can be invaluable to new and existing users alike. Unlike the brief "Usage" heading in the README in **Section 6.2.1**, these examples are more like tutorials, including a mix of text, figures, and code that demonstrate the functionality and common workflows of your package step-by-step. The examples should be realistic and illustrate workflows that users of your package might actually do (as opposed to toy examples).

It's important to think about your audience here too. Sometimes, it's necessary to create examples for different levels of expertise. Examples for new users will introduce the basic functionality of your package step-by-step, with plenty of commentary about what each piece of code is doing and why. Examples for more competent users might be more code-based, requiring less explanation of each step, and will likely explore more advanced usage of the package.

You could certainly write examples from scratch using a plain-text format like Markdown, but this can be inefficient and prone to errors. Instead, we recommend creating examples using a computational notebook like a Jupyter Notebook (Kluyver et al., 2016) (*.ipynb* file). Jupyter Notebooks are interactive documents that can contain code, equations, text, and visualizations.

They are effective for demonstrating examples because they directly import and use code from your package; this ensures you don't make mistakes when writing out your example, and it allows users to download, execute, and interact with the notebooks themselves (as opposed to just reading text).

To create examples in a Jupyter notebook, you'll need to install the Jupyter software. If you're using a poetry-managed project, as we do in this book, you can install the Jupyter software as a development dependency of your package with the following command:

> If you're following on from **Chapter 3: How to package a Python** and created a virtual environment for your pycounts package using conda, as we did in **Section 3.5.1**, be sure to activate that environment before continuing by running conda activate pycounts at the command line.

```
$ poetry add --dev jupyter
```

Once installed, you can launch the Jupyter Notebook application with the following command:

```
$ jupyter notebook
```

> If you're developing your Python package in an IDE that natively supports Jupyter Notebooks, such as Visual Studio Code or JupyterLab, you can simply open *docs/example.ipynb* to edit it, without needing to run the jupyter notebook command above.

Notebooks are made of "cells" that can contain Python code or Markdown text. Discussing how to use the Jupyter application is beyond the scope of this book, and we refer readers to the Jupyter documentation[12] to learn more.

---

[12] https://jupyter-notebook.readthedocs.io/en/latest/?badge=latest

However, as an example, Fig. 6.2 and Fig. 6.3 show the example notebook that we created to support our `pycounts` package in **Section 3.8.3**.

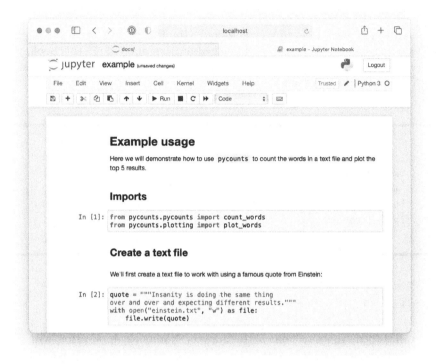

FIGURE 6.2: First half of Jupyter Notebook demonstrating an example workflow using the pycounts package.

In **Section 3.8.4**, we'll show how we can use `sphinx` to automatically execute notebooks and include their content (including the outputs of code cells) into our built documentation so that users can easily read and navigate through them without having to even start the Jupyter application!

6.2.7 Docstrings

A docstring is a string, surrounded by triple-quotes, at the start of a module, class, or function in Python (preceding any code) that provides documentation on what the object does and how to use it. Docstrings automatically become the documented object's documentation, accessible to users via the `help()` function. Docstrings are a user's first port-of-call when they are trying to use code from your package; they really are a necessity when creating packages, even for yourself.

General docstring convention in Python is described in Python Enhancement

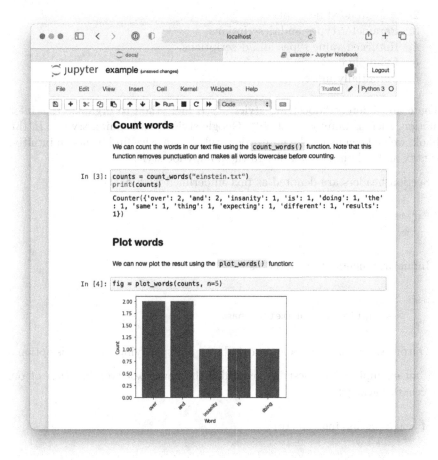

FIGURE 6.3: Second half of Jupyter Notebook demonstrating an example workflow using the pycounts package.

Proposal (PEP) 257 — Docstring Conventions[13], but there is flexibility in how you write your docstrings. A minimal docstring contains a single line describing what the object does, and that might be sufficient for a simple function or for when your code is in the early stages of development. However, for code you intend to share with others (including your future self) a more comprehensive docstring should be written.

A typical docstring will include:

1. A one-line summary that does not use variable names or the function name.

---

[13]https://www.python.org/dev/peps/pep-0257/

2. An extended description.
3. Parameter types and descriptions.
4. Returned value types and descriptions.
5. Example usage.
6. Potentially more.

There are different "docstring styles" used in Python to organize this information, such as numpydoc style[14], Google style[15], and sphinx style[16]. In this book, we've been using the numpydoc style because we find it has an intuitive syntax and is human-readable. In the numpydoc style:

- Section headers are denoted as text underlined with dashes:

```
Parameters
----------
```

- Input arguments are denoted as:

```
name : type
    Description of parameter `name`.
```

- Output values use the same syntax above, but specifying the name is optional.

As an example of a docstring, consider the count_words() function of our pycounts package:

```
def count_words(input_file):
    """Count words in a text file.

    Words are made lowercase and punctuation is removed
    before counting.

    Parameters
    ----------
    input_file : str
        Path to text file.

    Returns
    -------
    collections.Counter
```

---

[14]https://numpydoc.readthedocs.io/en/latest/format.html#docstring-standard
[15]https://github.com/google/styleguide/blob/gh-pages/pyguide.md#38-comments-and-docstrings
[16]https://sphinx-rtd-tutorial.readthedocs.io/en/latest/docstrings.html#the-sphinx-docstring-format

```
        dict-like object where keys are words and values are counts.

    Examples
    --------
    >>> count_words("text.txt")
    """
    text = load_text(input_file)
    text = clean_text(text)
    words = text.split()
    return Counter(words)
```

You can add information to your docstrings at your discretion — you won't always need all the sections above, and in some case you may want to include additional sections from the numpydoc style documentation[17].

6.2.8 Application programming interface (API) reference

An application programming interface (API) reference sheet is an organized index of your package's user-facing functionality and associated docstrings. It helps users efficiently understand and search through your package's functionality without having to dig in to the source code or run the Python `help()` command on every object they need to know about.

As a concrete example of what we're talking about, Fig. 6.4 shows an API reference for our `pycounts` package, and Fig. 6.5 shows the detail we get when we click on the `pycounts.plotting` module.

You could create an API reference by manually copying and pasting the names of all of your package's Python objects (functions, modules, classes, etc.) and their docstrings into a plain-text file, but that would be incredibly tedious and not reproducible. Instead, API references are usually generated automatically using `sphinx`, which can parse your source code to extract Python objects and their docstrings and render them into an API reference. We'll demonstrate how to do this in **Section 3.8.4**.

6.2.9 Other package documentation

In this section, we've only explored the core documentation typically included in a Python package. But you can add as much documentation as you wish! For example, you might wish to write documents for frequently asked questions (FAQs), a document referencing how your project compares to similar projects, information on project funding and attribution, etc. In general, the more documentation the better!

---

[17]https://numpydoc.readthedocs.io/en/latest/format.html#docstring-standard

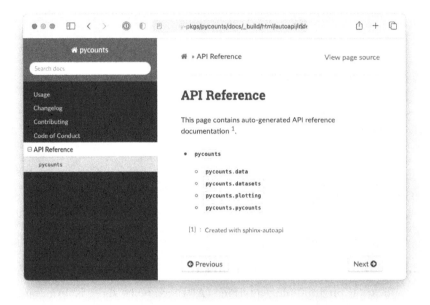

FIGURE 6.4: API reference for the pycounts package.

6.3   Building documentation

At the moment, the documentation we've written is spread throughout our package's directory structure in the form of plain-text Markdown files, Jupyter Notebooks, and docstrings in our Python modules. Rather than requiring users to search through this directory structure to find documentation, it's common to use a documentation generator like sphinx to compile and render all of this plain-text documentation into a user-friendly output format, such as HTML or PDF, that is easy to view, navigate, and share with others. We showed an example of sphinx-generated documentation in Fig. 6.1. As we'll see in this section, sphinx also has a rich ecosystem of extensions that can be used to help customize and automatically generate content to complement your manually-written documentation.

We'll demonstrate the process of building documentation with sphinx using our pycounts package. This section will effectively walk through the same steps we went through in **Section 3.8.4**, so for readers who have recently read that section, feel free to skip to **Section 3.8.5**.

FIGURE 6.5: API reference for the pycounts.plotting package.

The source and configuration files to build documentation using sphinx live in a *docs/* folder in the root of your package. The py-pkgs-cookiecutter automatically created this folder for us:

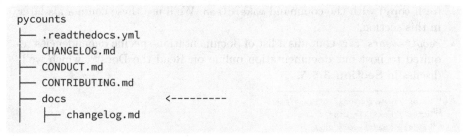

```
pycounts
├── .readthedocs.yml
├── CHANGELOG.md
├── CONDUCT.md
├── CONTRIBUTING.md
├── docs              <---------
│   ├── changelog.md
```

```
        ├── conduct.md
        ├── conf.py
        ├── contributing.md
        ├── example.ipynb
        ├── index.md
        ├── make.bat
        ├── Makefile
        └── requirements.txt
    ├── LICENSE
    ├── pyproject.toml
    ├── README.md
    ├── src
    │   └── ...
    └── tests
        └── ...
```

If you don't use a template to create your Python package directory structure, the sphinx command sphinx-quickstart can be used to quickly create the source files in the *docs/* directory for you.

The *docs/* directory includes:

- *Makefile/make.bat*: files that contain commands needed to build our documentation with sphinx and do not need to be modified. Make[18] is a tool used to run commands to efficiently read, process, and write files. A Makefile defines the tasks for Make to execute. If you're interested in learning more about Make, we recommend the Learn Makefiles[19] tutorial. But for building documentation with sphinx, all you need to know is that having these Makefiles allows us to build documentation with the simple command make html and to clean documentation (i.e., remove it so we can make a fresh copy) with the command make clean. We'll use these commands later in this section.
- *requirements.txt*: contains a list of documentation-specific dependencies required to host our documentation online on Read the Docs[20], which we'll discuss in **Section 3.8.5**.

---

[18]https://www.gnu.org/software/make/
[19]https://makefiletutorial.com
[20]https://readthedocs.org/

- `conf.py` is a configuration file controlling how `sphinx` builds your documentation. You can read more about `conf.py` in the `sphinx` documentation[21], and we'll touch on it again shortly, but for now, it has been pre-populated by the `py-pkgs-cookiecutter` template and does not need to be modified.
- The remaining files in the `docs/` directory form the content of our generated documentation, as we'll discuss in the remainder of this section.

The `index.md` file will form the landing page of our documentation. Think of it as the homepage of a website. For your landing page, you'd typically want some high-level information about your package, and then links to the rest of the documentation you want to expose to a user. For example, the landing page we are going to build will look like Fig. 6.6.

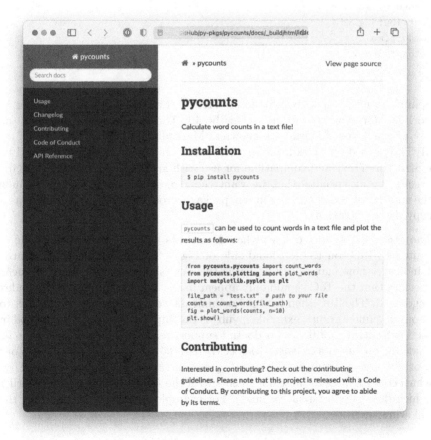

FIGURE 6.6: The documentation homepage generated by sphinx.

---

[21]https://www.sphinx-doc.org/en/master/usage/configuration.html

If you open *index.md* in an editor of your choice you'll see we're generating this content with a particular kind of syntax explained below.

```
```{include} ../README.md
```
```

```
```toctree
:maxdepth: 1
:hidden:

example.ipynb
changelog.md
contributing.md
conduct.md
autoapi/index
```
```

Sphinx natively supports reStructuredText[22], but many developers prefer to work in Markdown (as we do in this book). The syntax shown above in *index.md* is a flavor of Markdown known as Markedly Structured Text (MyST)[23]. MyST is based on Markdown but with additional syntax options inspired by reStructuredText and compatible for use with sphinx. For example, the {include} syntax specifies that we want the *index.md* landing page to include the content of the *README.md* in our package's root directory (think of it as a copy-paste operation).

The {toctree} syntax defines what documents will be listed in the table of contents (ToC) on the left-hand side of Fig. 6.6. The argument :maxdepth: 1 indicates how many heading levels the ToC should include, and :hidden: specifies that the ToC should only appear in the side bar and not in the index page itself. The ToC then lists the documents we want to include and link to in our documentation. "example.ipynb" is the Jupyter Notebook we showed in section **Section 6.2.6**. sphinx doesn't support relative links in a ToC, so to include the documents *CHANGELOG.md*, *CONTRIBUTING.md*, and *CONDUCT.md* from our root, we create "stub files" *changelog.md*, *contributing.md*, and *conduct.md*, which contain links to these documents with the {include} syntax from earlier (which does support relative links). For example, *changelog.md* contains the following text:

```
```{include} ../CHANGELOG.md
```
```

---

[22]https://www.sphinx-doc.org/en/master/usage/restructuredtext/index.html
[23]https://myst-parser.readthedocs.io/en/latest/syntax/syntax.html

The final document in the ToC, "autoapi/index" is an API reference sheet that will be generated automatically for us, from our package structure and docstrings, when we build our documentation with sphinx.

Before we can go ahead and build our documentation with sphinx, it relies on a few sphinx extensions that need to be installed and configured:

- myst-nb[24]: extension that enables sphinx to parse Markdown, MyST, and notebook files (sphinx only supports reStructuredTex, *.rst* files, by default).
- sphinx-rtd-theme[25]: a custom theme for styling the way our documentation will look. It looks much better than the sphinx default.
- sphinx-autoapi[26]: extension that will parse our source code and docstrings to create an API reference sheet.
- sphinx.ext.napoleon[27]: enables sphinx to parse numpydoc style docstrings.
- sphinx.ext.viewcode[28]: adds a helpful link to the source code of each object in the API reference sheet.

These extensions are not necessary to create documentation with sphinx, but they are all commonly used in Python packaging documentation and significantly improve the look and user-experience of the generated documentation. Extensions without the sphinx.ext prefix need to be installed. We can install them as development dependencies in a poetry-managed project with the following command:

```
$ poetry add --dev myst-nb --python "^3.9"
$ poetry add --dev sphinx-autoapi sphinx-rtd-theme
```

Adding myst-nb is a great example of why upper caps on dependency versions can be a pain, as we discussed in **Section 3.6.1**. At the time of writing, one of the dependencies of myst-nb, mdit-py-plugins, has an upper cap of <4.0 on the Python version it requires, so it's not compatible with our package which supports Python >=3.9. Thus, unless mdit-py-plugins removes this upper cap, the easiest way for us to add myst-nb is to tell poetry to only install it for Python versions ^3.9 (i.e., >=3.9 and <4.0), by using the argument --python "^3.9".

---

[24]https://myst-nb.readthedocs.io/en/latest/
[25]https://sphinx-rtd-theme.readthedocs.io/en/stable/
[26]https://sphinx-autoapi.readthedocs.io/en/latest/
[27]https://sphinxcontrib-napoleon.readthedocs.io/en/latest/
[28]https://www.sphinx-doc.org/en/master/usage/extensions/viewcode.html

Once installed, any extensions you want to use need to be added to a list called extensions in the *conf.py* configuration file and configured. Configuration options for each extension (if they exist) can be viewed in their respective documentation, but the py-pkgs-cookeicutter has already taken care of everything for us, by defining the following variables within *conf.py*:

```
extensions = [
    "myst_nb",
    "autoapi.extension",
    "sphinx.ext.napoleon",
    "sphinx.ext.viewcode",
]
autoapi_dirs = ["../src"]  # location to parse for API reference
html_theme = "sphinx_rtd_theme"
```

With our documentation structure set up, and our extensions configured, we can now navigate to the *docs/* directory and build our documentation with sphinx using the following commands:

```
$ cd docs
$ make html
```

```
Running Sphinx
...
build succeeded.
The HTML pages are in _build/html.
```

If we now look inside our *docs/* directory we see a new directory *_build/html*, which contains our built documentation as HTML files. If you open *_build/html/index.html* you should see the landing page in Fig. 6.6.

If you make significant changes to your documentation, it can be a good idea to delete the *_build/* folder before building it again. You can do this easily by adding the clean option into the make html command: make clean html.

The sphinx-autoapi and sphinx.ext.napoleon extensions extracted the docstrings within each module and rendered them into our documentation. If you click "API Reference" you should now be able to view pages like those shown in Fig. 6.4 and Fig. 6.5.

If you navigate to the "Example usage" page, you should see a rendered version of our Jupyter Notebook example, as shown in Fig. 6.7. This was made possible using the `myst-nb` extension.

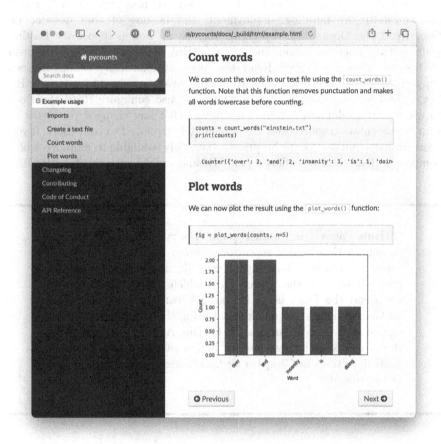

FIGURE 6.7: Jupyter Notebook example rendered into pycounts's documentation.

Ultimately, you can efficiently make beautiful and many-featured documentation with `sphinx` and its ecosystem of extensions. You can now use this documentation yourself or potentially share it with others, but it really shines when you host it on the web using a free service like Read the Docs[29], as we'll do in the next section.

---

[29]https://readthedocs.org/

6.4   Hosting documentation online

If you intend to share your package with others, it will be useful to make your documentation accessible online. It's common to host Python package documentation on the free online hosting service Read the Docs[30], which can automate the building, deployment, and hosting of your documentation. Read the Docs works by connecting to an online repository hosting your package documentation, such as a GitHub repository. When you push changes to your repository, Read the Docs automatically builds a fresh copy of your documentation (i.e., runs `make html`) and hosts it at the URL `https://pkgname.readthedocs.io/` (you can also configure Read the Docs to use a custom domain name). This means that any changes you make to your documentation source files are immediately deployed to your users. If you need your documentation to be private (i.e., only available to employees of a company), Read the Docs offers a paid "Business plan" with this functionality.

GitHub Pages[31] is another popular service used for hosting documentation from a repository. However, it doesn't natively support automatic building of your documentation when you push changes to the source files, which is why we prefer to use Read the Docs here. If you did want to host your docs on GitHub Pages, we recommend using the ghp-import[32] package, or setting up an automated GitHub Actions workflow using the peaceiris/actions-gh-pages[33] action (we'll learn more about GitHub Actions in **Chapter 8: Continuous integration and deployment**).

The Read the Docs[34] documentation will provide the most up-to-date steps required to host your documentation online. For our `pycounts` package, this involved the following steps:

1. Visit `https://readthedocs.org/` and click on "Sign up".
2. Select "Sign up with GitHub".

---

[30]`https://readthedocs.org/`
[31]`https://pages.github.com`
[32]`https://github.com/c-w/ghp-import`
[33]`https://github.com/peaceiris/actions-gh-pages`
[34]`https://readthedocs.org`

3. Click "Import a Project".
4. Click "Import Manually".
5. Fill in the project details by:
   - Providing your package name (e.g., `pycounts`).
   - The GitHub repository URL (e.g., `https://github.com/Tomas Beuzen/pycounts`).
   - Specifying the default branch as `main`.
6. Click "Next" and then "Build version".

After following the steps above, your documentation should be successfully built by Read the Docs[35], and you should be able to access it via the "View Docs" button on the build page. For example, the documentation for `pycounts` is now available at `https://pycounts.readthedocs.io/en/latest/`. This documentation will be automatically re-built by Read the Docs each time you push changes to the specified default branch of your GitHub repository.

The `.readthedocs.yml` file that `py-pkgs-cookiecutter` created for us in the root directory of our Python package contains the configuration settings necessary for Read the Docs to properly build our documentation. It specifies what version of Python to use and tells Read the Docs that our documentation requires the extra packages specified in `pycounts/docs/requirements.txt` to be generated correctly.

---

[35] `https://readthedocs.org/`

7

Releasing and versioning

Previous chapters have focused on how to develop a Python package from scratch by creating the Python source code, developing a testing framework, writing documentation, and then releasing it online via PyPI (if desired). This chapter now describes the next step in the packaging workflow — updating your package!

At any given time, your package's users (including you) will install a particular version of your package in a project. If you change the package's source code, their code could potentially break (imagine you change a module name, or remove a function argument a user was using). To solve this problem, developers assign a unique version number to each unique state of their package and release each new version independently. Most of the time, users will want to use the most up-to-date version of your package, but sometimes, they'll need to use an older version that is compatible with their project. Releasing versions is also an important way of communicating to your users that your package has changed (e.g., bugs have been fixed, new features have been added, etc.).

In this chapter, we'll walk through the process of creating and releasing new versions of your Python package.

7.1 Version numbering

Versioning is the process of adding unique identifiers to different versions of your package. The unique identifier you use may be name-based or number-based, but most Python packages use semantic versioning[1]. In semantic versioning, a version number consists of three integers A.B.C, where A is the "major" version, B is the "minor" version, and C is the "patch" version. The first version of a software usually starts at 0.1.0 and increments from there. We call an increment a "bump", and it consists of adding 1 to either the major, minor, or patch identifier as follows:

- **Patch** release (0.1.0 -> 0.1.1): patch releases are typically used for bug fixes, which are backward compatible. Backward compatibility refers to the

---

[1]https://semver.org

DOI: 10.1201/9781003189251-7

compatibility of your package with previous versions of itself. For example, if a user was using v0.1.0 of your package, they should be able to upgrade to v0.1.1 and have any code they previously wrote still work. It's fine to have so many patch releases that you need to use two digits (e.g., 0.1.27).

- **Minor** release (0.1.0 -> 0.**2**.0): a minor release typically includes larger bug fixes or new features that are backward compatible, for example, the addition of a new function. It's fine to have so many minor releases that you need to use two digits (e.g., 0.13.0).
- **Major** release (0.1.0 -> **1**.0.0): release 1.0.0 is typically used for the first stable release of your package. After that, major releases are made for changes that are not backward compatible and may affect many users. Changes that are not backward compatible are called "breaking changes". For example, changing the name of one of the modules in your package would be a breaking change; if users upgraded to your new package, any code they'd written using the old module name would no longer work, and they would have to change it.

Most of the time, you'll be making patch and minor releases. We'll discuss major releases, breaking changes, and how to deprecate package functionality (i.e., remove it) more in **Section 7.5**.

Even with the guidelines above, versioning a package can be a little subjective and requires you to use your best judgment. For example, small packages might make a patch release for each individual bug fixed or a minor release for each new feature added. In contrast, larger packages will often group multiple bug fixes into a single patch release or multiple features into a single minor release, because making a release for every individual change would result in an overwhelming and confusing amount of releases! Table 7.1 shows some practical examples of major, minor, and patch releases made for the Python software itself. To formalize the circumstances under which different kinds of releases should be made, some developers create a "version policy" document for their package; the pandas version policy[2] is a good example of this.

---

[2]https://pandas.pydata.org/docs/development/policies.html#version-policy

TABLE 7.1: Examples of major, minor, and patch releases of Python.

Release Type	Version Bump	Description
Major	2.X.X -> 3.0.0 (December, 2008)	This release included breaking changes, e.g., `print()` became a function, integer division resulted a float rather than an integer, built-in objects like dictionaries and strings changed considerably, and many old features were removed.
Minor	3.8.X -> 3.9.0 (October, 2020)	New features and optimizations were added in this release, e.g., string methods to remove prefixes and suffixes (`.removeprefix()`/`.removesuffix()`) were added, and a new parser was implemented for CPython (the engine that compiles and executes your Python code).
Patch	3.9.5 -> 3.9.6 (June, 2021)	This release contained bug and maintenance fixes, e.g., a confusing error message was updated in the `str.format()` method, and the version of `pip` bundled with Python downloads was updated from 21.1.2 -> 21.1.3, and parts of the documentation were updated.

7.2   Version bumping

While we'll discuss the full workflow for releasing a new version of your package in **Section 7.3**, we first want to dicuss version bumping. That is, how to increment the version of your package when you're preparing a new release. This can be done manually or automatically as we'll show below.

7.2.1   Manual version bumping

Once you've decided what the new version of your package will be (i.e., are you making a patch, minor, or major release) you need to update the package's version number in your source code. For a `poetry`-managed project, that information is in the `pyproject.toml` file. Consider the `pyproject.toml` file of the pycounts package we developed in **Chapter 3: How to package a Python**, the top of which looks like this:

```
[tool.poetry]
name = "pycounts"
version = "0.1.0"
description = "Calculate word counts in a text file!"
authors = ["Tomas Beuzen"]
license = "MIT"
readme = "README.md"
```

...rest of file hidden...

Imagine we wanted to make a patch release of our package. We could simply change the `version` number manually in this file to "0.1.1", and many developers do take this manual approach. An alternative method is to use the `poetry version` command. The `poetry version` command can be used with the arguments `patch`, `minor`, or `major` depending on how you want to update the version of your package. For example, to make a patch release, we could run the following at the command line:

If you're building the `pycounts` package with us in this book, you don't have to run the below command, it is just for demonstration purposes. We'll make a new version of `pycounts` later in this chapter.

```
$ poetry version patch
```

```
Bumping version from 0.1.0 to 0.1.1
```

This command changes the `version` variable in the `pyproject.toml` file:

```
[tool.poetry]
name = "pycounts"
version = "0.1.1"
description = "Calculate word counts in a text file!"
authors = ["Tomas Beuzen"]
license = "MIT"
readme = "README.md"

...rest of file hidden...
```

7.2.2   Automatic version bumping

In this book, we're interested in automating as much as possible of the packaging workflow. While the manual versioning approach described above in **Section 7.2.1** is certainly used by many developers, we can do things more efficiently! To automate version bumping, you'll need to be using a version control system like Git. If you are not using version control for your package, you can skip to **Section 7.3**.

Python Semantic Release (PSR)[3] is a tool that can automatically bump version numbers based on keywords it finds in commit messages. The idea is to use a standardized commit message format and syntax, which PSR can parse to determine how to increment the version number. The default commit message format used by PSR is the Angular commit style[4], which looks like this:

```
<type>(optional scope): short summary in present tense

(optional body: explains motivation for the change)

(optional footer: note BREAKING CHANGES here, and issues to be closed)
```

---

[3]https://python-semantic-release.readthedocs.io/en/latest/
[4]https://github.com/angular/angular.js/blob/master/DEVELOPERS.md#commit-message-format

<type> refers to the kind of change made and is usually one of:

- feat: A new feature.
- fix: A bug fix.
- docs: Documentation changes.
- style: Changes that do not affect the meaning of the code (white-space, formatting, missing semi-colons, etc).
- refactor: A code change that neither fixes a bug nor adds a feature.
- perf: A code change that improves performance.
- test: Changes to the test framework.
- build: Changes to the build process or tools.

scope is an optional keyword that provides context for where the change was made. It can be anything relevant to your package or development workflow (e.g., it could be the module or function name affected by the change).

Different text in the commit message will trigger PSR to make different kinds of releases:

- A <type> of fix triggers a patch version bump, e.g.:

```
$ git commit -m "fix(mod_plotting): fix confusing error message in \
                 plot_words"
```

- A <type> of feat triggers a minor version bump, e.g.:

```
$ git commit -m "feat(package): add example data and new module to \
                 package"
```

- The text BREAKING CHANGE: in the footer will trigger a major release, e.g.:

```
$ git commit -m "feat(mod_plotting): move code from plotting module \
                 to pycounts module
$
$ BREAKING CHANGE: plotting module wont exist after this release."
```

To use PSR we need to install and configure it. To install PSR as a development dependency of a poetry-managed project, you can use the following command:

```
$ poetry add --dev python-semantic-release
```

To configure PSR, we need to tell it where the version number of our package is stored. The package version is stored in the *pyproject.toml* file for a poetry-managed project. It exists as the variable version under the table [tool.poetry]. To tell PSR this, we need to add a new table to the *pypro-ject.toml* file called [tool.semantic_release] within which we specify that our version_variable is stored at pyproject.toml:version:

...rest of file hidden...

```
[tool.semantic_release]
version_variable = "pyproject.toml:version"
```

Finally, you can use the command semantic-release version at the command line to get PSR to automatically bump your package's version number. PSR will parse all the commit messages since the last tag of your package to determine what kind of version bump to make. For example, imagine the following three commit messages have been made since tag v0.1.0:

1. "fix(mod_plotting): raise TypeError in plot_words"
2. "fix(mod_plotting): fix confusing error message in plot_words"
3. "feat(package): add example data and new module to package"

PSR will note that there are two "fix" and one "feat" keywords. "fix" triggers a patch release, but "feat" triggers a minor release, which trumps a patch release, so PSR would make a minor version bump from v0.1.0 to v0.2.0.

As a more practical demonstration of how PSR works, imagine we have a package at version 0.1.0, make a bug fix and commit our changes with the following message:

If you're building the pycounts package with us in this book, you don't have to run the below commands, they are just for demonstration purposes. We'll make a new version of pycounts later in this chapter.

```
$ git add src/pycounts/plotting.py
$ git commit -m "fix(code): change confusing error message in \
  plotting.plot_words"
```

We then run semantic-release version to update our version number. In the command below, we'll specify the argument -v DEBUG to ask PSR to print extra information to the screen so we can get an inside look at how PSR works:

```
$ semantic-release version -v DEBUG


Creating new version
debug: get_current_version_by_config_file()
debug: Parsing current version: path=PosixPath('pyproject.toml')
debug: Regex matched version: 0.1.0
debug: get_current_version_by_config_file -> 0.1.0
Current version: 0.1.0
debug: evaluate_version_bump('0.1.0', None)
debug: parse_commit_message('fix(code): change confusing error... )
debug: parse_commit_message -> ParsedCommit(bump=1, type='fix')
debug: Commits found since last release: 1
debug: evaluate_version_bump -> patch
debug: get_new_version('0.1.0', 'patch')
debug: get_new_version -> 0.1.1
debug: set_new_version('0.1.1')
debug: Writing new version number: path=PosixPath('pyproject.toml')
debug: set_new_version -> True
debug: commit_new_version('0.1.1')
debug: commit_new_version -> [main d82fa3f] 0.1.1
debug:   Author: semantic-release <semantic-release>
debug:   1 file changed, 5 insertions(+), 1 deletion(-)
debug: tag_new_version('0.1.1')
debug: tag_new_version ->
Bumping with a patch version to 0.1.1
```

We can see that PSR found our commit messages, and decided that a patch release was necessary based on the text in the message. We can also see that command automatically updated the version number in the the *pyproject.toml* file and created a new version control tag for our package's source (we talked about tags in **Section 3.9**). In the next section, we'll go through a real example of using PSR with our pycounts package.

7.3   Checklist for releasing a new package version

Now that we know about versioning and how to increment the version of our package, we're ready to run through a release checklist. We'll make a new minor release of the pycounts package we've been developing throughout this book, from v0.1.0 to v0.2.0, to demonstrate each step in the release checklist.

7.3.1 Step 1: make changes to package source files

This is an obvious one, but before you can make a new release, you need to make the changes to your package's source that will comprise your new release!

Consider our pycounts package. We published the first release, v0.1.0, of our package in **Chapter 3: How to package a Python**. Since then, we've made a few changes. Specifically:

- In **Chapter 4: Package structure and distribution**, we added a new "datasets" module to our package along with some example data, a text file of the novel *Flatland* by Edwin Abbott (Abbott, 1884), that users could load to try out the functionality of our package.
- In **Chapter 5: Testing**, we significantly upgraded our testing suite by adding several new unit, integration, and regression tests to the *tests/test_pycounts.py* file.

In practice, if you're using version control, changes are usually made to a package's source using branches[5]. Branches isolate your changes so you can develop your package without affecting the existing, stable version. Only when you're happy with your changes do you merge them into the existing source.

7.3.2 Step 2: document your changes

Before we make our new release, we should document everything we've changed in our changelog. For example, here's pycounts's updated *CHANGELOG.md* file:

We talked about changelog file format and content in **Section 6.2.5**.

---

[5]https://git-scm.com/book/en/v2/Git-Branching-Branches-in-a-Nutshell

```
# Changelog

<!--next-version-placeholder-->

## v0.2.0 (10/09/2021)

### Feature

- Added new datasets modules to load example data

### Fix

- Check type of argument passed to `plotting.plot_words()`

### Tests

- Added new tests to all package modules in test_pycounts.py

## v0.1.0 (24/08/2021)

- First release of `pycounts`
```

If using version control, you should commit this change to make sure it becomes part of your release:

```
$ git add CHANGELOG.md
$ git commit -m "build: preparing for release v0.2.0"
$ git push
```

7.3.3 Step 3: bump version number

Once your changes for the new release are ready, you need to bump the package version manually (**Section 7.2.1**) or automatically with the PSR tool (**Section 7.2.2**).

We'll take the automatic route using PSR here, but if you're not using Git as a version control system, you'll need to do this step manually. The changes we made to pycounts, described in the section above, constitute a minor release (we added a new feature to load example data and made some significant changes to our package's test framework). When we committed these changes in **Section** 4.4 and **Section** 4.4, we did so with the following collection of commit messages:

```
$ git commit -m "feat: add example data and datasets module"
$ git commit -m "test: add additional tests for all modules"
$ git commit -m "fix: check input type to plot_words function"
```

As we discussed in **Section 7.2.2**, PSR can automatically parse these commit messages to increment our package version for us. If you haven't already, install PSR as a development dependency using `poetry`:

If you're following on from **Chapter 3: How to package a Python** and created a virtual environment for your `pycounts` package using `conda`, as we did in **Section 3.5.1**, be sure to activate that environment before continuing by running `conda activate pycounts` at the command line.

```
$ poetry add --dev python-semantic-release
```

This command updated our recorded package dependencies in `pyproject.toml` and `poetry.lock`, so we should commit those changes to version control before we update our package version:

```
$ git add pyproject.toml poetry.lock
$ git commit -m "build: add PSR as dev dependency"
$ git push
```

Now we can use PSR to automatically bump our package version with the `semantic-release version` command. If you want to see exactly what PSR found in your commit messages and why it decided to make a patch, minor, or major release, you can add the argument `-v DEBUG`.

Recall from **Section 7.2.2** that to use PSR, you need to tell it where your package's version number is stored by defining `version_variable = "pyproject.toml:version"` under the `[tool.semantic_release]` table in *pyproject.toml*.

```
$ semantic-release version
```

```
Creating new version
Current version: 0.1.0
Bumping with a minor version to 0.2.0
```

This step automatically updated our package's version in the *pyproject.toml* file and created a new tag for our package, "v0.2.0", which you could view by typing `git tag --list` at the command line:

```
$ git tag --list
```

```
v0.1.0
v0.2.0
```

7.3.4   Step 4: run tests and build documentation

We've now prepped our package for release, but before we release it, it's important to check that its tests run and documentation builds successfully. To do this with our `pycounts` package, we should first install the package (we should re-install because we've created a new version):

```
$ poetry install
```

Installing the current project: pycounts (0.2.0)

Now we'll check that our tests are still passing and what their coverage is using `pytest` and `pytest-cov` (we discussed these tools in **Chapter 5: Testing**):

```
$ pytest tests/ --cov=pycounts
```

```
========================== test session starts ==========================

----------- coverage: platform darwin, python 3.9.6-final-0 -----------
Name                             Stmts   Miss  Cover
---------------------------------------------------------
src/pycounts/__init__.py             2      0   100%
src/pycounts/data/__init__.py        0      0   100%
```

```
src/pycounts/datasets.py        5       0     100%
src/pycounts/plotting.py        12      0     100%
src/pycounts/pycounts.py        16      0     100%
--------------------------------------------------------
TOTAL                           35      0     100%

========================= 7 passed in 0.41s =========================
```

Finally, to check that documentation still builds correctly you typically want to create the documentation from scratch, i.e., remove any existing built documentation in your package and then building it again. To do this, we first need to run make clean before running make html from the *docs/* directory (we discussed building documentation with these commands in **Chapter 6: Documentation**). In the spirit of efficiency we can combine these two commands together like we do below:

```
$ cd docs
$ make clean html
```

```
Running Sphinx
...
build succeeded.
The HTML pages are in _build/html.
```

Looks like everything is working!

7.3.5   Step 5: tag a release with version control

For those using remote version control on GitHub (or similar), it's time to tag a new release of your repository on GitHub. If you're not using version control, you can skip to the next section. We discussed how to tag a release and why we do this in **Section 3.9**. Recall that it's a two-step process:

1. Create a tag marking a specific point in a repository's history using the command git tag.
2. On GitHub, create a release of your repository based on the tag.

If using PSR to bump your package version, then step 1 was done automatically for you. If you didn't use PSR, you can make a tag manually using the following command:

```
$ git tag v0.2.0
```

You can now push any local commits and your new tag to GitHub with the
following commands:

```
$ git push
$ git push --tags
```

After running those commands for our pycounts package, we can go to GitHub
and navigate to the "Releases" tab to see our tag, as shown in Fig. 7.1.

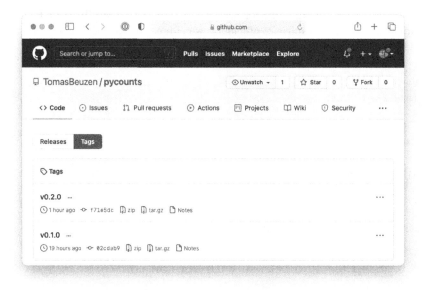

FIGURE 7.1: Tag of v0.2.0 of pycounts on GitHub.

To create a release from this tag, click "Draft a new release". You can then
identify the tag from which to create the release and optionally add a description of the release; often, this description links to the changelog, where
changes have already been documented. Fig. 7.2 shows the release of v0.2.0 of
pycounts on GitHub.

7.3.6   Step 6: build and release package to PyPI

It's now time to build the new distributions for our package (i.e., the sdist
and wheel — we talked about these in **Section** 4.3). We can do that with
poetry using the following command run from the root package directory:

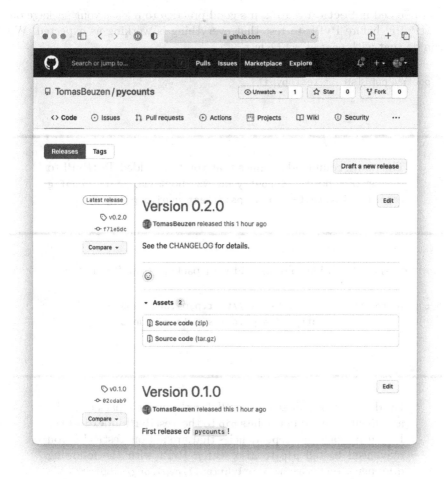

FIGURE 7.2: Release v0.2.0 of pycounts on GitHub.

```
$ poetry build
```

```
Building pycounts (0.2.0)
  - Building sdist
  - Built pycounts-0.2.0.tar.gz
  - Building wheel
  - Built pycounts-0.2.0-py3-none-any.whl
```

You can now use and share these distributions as you please, but most developers will want to upload them to PyPI, which is what we'll do here.

As discussed in **Section 3.10.2**, it's good practice to release your package on TestPyPI[6] before PyPI, to test that everything is working as expected. We can do that with `poetry publish`:

```
$ poetry publish -r test-pypi
```

The above command assumes that you have added TestPyPI to the list of repositories `poetry` knows about via: `poetry config repositories.test-pypi https://test.pypi.org/legacy/`

Now you should be able to download your package from TestPyPI:

```
$ pip install --index-url https://test.pypi.org/simple/ \
  --extra-index-url https://pypi.org/simple pycounts
```

By default `pip` will search PyPI for the named package. The argument `--index-url` points `pip` to the TestPyPI index instead. If your package has dependencies that are not on TestPyPI, you may need to tell `pip` to also search PyPI with the following argument: `--extra-index-url https://pypi.org/simple`.

If you're happy with how your newly versioned package is working, you can go ahead and publish to PyPI:

```
$ poetry publish
```

---

[6]`https://test.pypi.org/`

7.4 Automating releases

As you've seen in this chapter, there are quite a few steps to go through in order to make a new release of a package. In **Chapter 8: Continuous integration and deployment** we'll see how we can automate the entire release process, including running tests, building documentation, and publishing to TestPyPI and PyPI.

7.5 Breaking changes and deprecating package functionality

As discussed earlier in the chapter, major version releases may come with backward incompatible changes, which we call "breaking changes". Breaking changes affect your package's user base. The impact and importance of breaking changes is directly proportional to the number of people using your package. That's not to say that you should avoid breaking changes — there are good reasons for making them, such as improving software design mistakes, improving functionality, or making code simpler and easier to use.

If you do need to make a breaking change, it is best to implement that change gradually, by providing adequate warning and advice to your package's user base through "deprecation warnings".

We can add a deprecation warning to our code by using the warnings module[7] from the Python standard library. For example, imagine that we want to remove the get_flatland() function from the datasets module of our pycounts package in the upcoming major v1.0.0 release. We can do this by adding a FutureWarning to our code, as shown in the *datasets.py* module below (we created this module back in **Section 4.2.6**).

If you've used any larger Python libraries before (such as NumPy, Pandas or scikit-learn) you probably have seen deprecation warnings before! On that note, these large, established Python libraries offer great resources for learning how to properly manage your own package — don't be afraid to check out their source code and history on GitHub.

---

[7]https://docs.python.org/3/library/warnings.html

```
from importlib import resources
import warnings

def get_flatland():
    """Get path to example "Flatland" [1]_ text file.

    ...rest of docstring hidden...
    """
    warnings.warn("This function will be deprecated in v1.0.0.",
                  FutureWarning)

    with resources.path("pycounts.data", "flatland.txt") as f:
        data_file_path = f
    return data_file_path
```

If we were to try and use this function now, we would see the `FutureWarning`
printed to our output:

```
>>> from pycounts.datasets import get_flatland
>>> flatland_path = get_flatland()
```

FutureWarning: This function will be deprecated in v1.0.0.

A few other things to think about when making breaking changes:

- If you're changing a function significantly, consider keeping both the legacy
  version (with a deprecation warning) and new version of the function for
  a few releases to help users make a smoother transition to using the new
  function.
- If you're deprecating a lot of code, consider doing it in small increments over
  multiple releases.
- If your breaking change is a result of one of your package's dependencies
  changing, it is often better to warn your users that they require a newer
  version of a dependency rather than immediately making it a required dependency of your package.
- Documentation is key! Don't be afraid to be verbose about documenting
  breaking changes in your package's documentation and changelog.

7.6 Updating dependency versions

If your package depends on other packages, like our `pycounts` package does, you'll need to think about updating your dependency version constraints as new versions of dependencies are released over time. This is true even for the version(s) of Python that your package supports.

Luckily, `poetry` makes this a relatively simple process. The command `poetry update` can be used to update the version of installed dependencies in your virtual environment, within the constraints of the *pyproject.toml* file. This is useful for testing that your package works as expected with newer versions of its dependencies. For example, if we wanted to install the latest version of `matplotlib` compatible with our `pycounts` package, we could use the following code:

```
$ poetry update matplotlib
```

However, `poetry update` won't update the constraints specified in your pyproject.toml file, or the metadata built into your package releases. To update that you have two options:

1. Manually modify version constraints in *pyproject.toml*.
2. Use `poetry add` to update a dependency to a specific version(s).

For example, our current version constraint for `matplotlib` is shown in *pyproject.toml*:

```
[tool.poetry.dependencies]
python = ">=3.9"
matplotlib = ">=3.4.3"
```

If we wanted the minimum version of `matplotlib` to now be 3.5.0, we could manually adjust our *pyproject.toml* file as shown below:

```
[tool.poetry.dependencies]
python = ">=3.9"
matplotlib = ">=3.5.0"
```

Or we could run the following code:

```
$ poetry add "matplotlib>=3.5.0"
```

We use double quotes in the command above because in many shells, like bash, > is a redirection operator. The double quotes are used to preserve the literal value of the contained characters (read more in the documentation[8]).

---

[8]http://www.gnu.org/software/bash/manual/html_node/Double-Quotes.html

8

Continuous integration and deployment

If you've gotten this far, you now have a working knowledge of how to create a fully-featured Python package! We went through quite a lot to get here: we learned about package structure, developed source code, created tests, wrote documentation, and learned how to release new versions of a package.

As you continue to develop your package into the future it would be helpful to automate many of these workflows so you and your collaborators can focus more on writing code and less on the nuances of packaging and testing. This is where continuous integration (CI) and continuous deployment (CD) come in! CI/CD generally refers to the automated testing, building, and deployment of software. In this chapter, we'll first introduce CI/CD and walk through how to set it up with the GitHub Actions service. After that, we'll show how to set up CI/CD for a Python package, demonstrating concepts using the pycounts package we've been developing throughout this book.

> This chapter requires basic familiarity with Git and GitHub or similar version control tools. To learn more about Git and GitHub, we recommend the following resources: *Happy Git and GitHub for the useR*[1] (Bryan et al., 2021) and *Research Software Engineering with Python*[2] (Irving et al., 2021).

8.1 An introduction to CI/CD

Continuous integration (CI) refers to the process of automatically evaluating your code as it is updated by yourself and contributors, to try and catch any potential issues your updates have caused. A CI workflow typically includes

---

[1]https://happygitwithr.com
[2]https://merely-useful.tech/py-rse/git-cmdline.html

automatic execution of many of the steps we've seen throughout this book, such as running tests, calculating code coverage, and building documentation, among others.

Continuous deployment (CD) is the process of automating the deployment of new versions of your software to e.g., PyPI, from changes that have made it through CI.

CI/CD can automate the packaging workflows that we've done manually throughout this book and can ultimately save you time and help you release new versions of your package quickly. CI/CD also helps others contribute to your package, because the process of updating your package is automated and doesn't depend on one person's expert knowledge (i.e., yours) of how to make releases manually. Even if your package won't be updated very often, setting up CI/CD is still beneficial because it means you don't have to remember all the manual steps required to make a release of your package (which can be daunting and deter you from wanting to update and maintain your package).

8.2　CI/CD tools

You could manually write and execute a CI/CD workflow by, for example, writing scripts that execute all of the steps we've walked through in previous chapters (i.e., running tests, building documented, build and release distributions, etc.). However, this process is not efficient or scalable, and it does not work well if more than one person (i.e., you) is contributing to your code.

It is therefore more common to use a CI/CD service to implement CI/CD. These services essentially do what we described above but in an automated manner; we define a workflow, which these services will automatically run at certain "trigger events", which we can also define (for example, merging new code into the "main" branch of a GitHub repository might trigger the automatic deployment of a new version of the software).

There are many CI/CD services out there — such as GitHub Actions[3], Travis CI[4], and CircleCi[5]. We'll be using GitHub Actions in this chapter, which is a service for executing CI/CD workflows for software stored in a GitHub repository. We'll introduce how to use GitHub Actions in the next section.

---

[3]https://docs.github.com/en/actions
[4]https://www.travis-ci.com
[5]https://circleci.com

GitHub Actions is free for public repositories and includes a generous amount of free minutes for private repositories. Read more in the GitHub Actions documentation[6].

8.3 Introduction to GitHub Actions

8.3.1 Key concepts

GitHub Actions is a service for executing CI/CD workflows. The general idea is to create a set of commands that GitHub Actions will run on our behalf. We call this set of commands a "workflow". A GitHub Actions workflow is defined in a *.yml* file and contains the set of "actions" we want GitHub Actions to run for us (such as running our tests with `pytest` or building our documentation with `sphinx`). Actions are organized as "steps" in a workflow (e.g., step 1: run tests, step 2: build documentation), which in turn are organized into "jobs" (e.g., job 1: continuous integration). A workflow is executed on a machine provided by GitHub Actions called a "runner", when triggered by a particular "event" (like merging code into the `main` branch of a repository).

That's a lot to take in, but don't worry! All this terminology is summarized in Table 8.1, and we'll walk through an example of using GitHub Actions, which refers to this terminology in the next section.

TABLE 8.1: Terminology used in GitHub Actions.

Keyword	Description
Actions	Individual tasks you want to perform.
Workflow	A collection of actions (specified together in one file).
Event	Something that triggers the running of a workflow.
Runner	A machine that can run the Github Action(s).
Job	A set of steps executed on the same runner.
Step	A set of commands or actions which a job executes.

---

[6]https://docs.github.com/en/billing/managing-billing-for-github-actions/about-billing-for-github-actions

8.3.2   A toy example

In this section, we'll walk through a simple example of running a workflow with GitHub Actions. The workflow will contains actions that simply print some things to the GitHub Actions runner's terminal using the `echo` command, when a change is made to a repository's content.

- **Step 1**

  Create a new repository on GitHub named anything you like (we called our repository "actions-example"). Click on the "Actions" tab, and then click the "Set up this workflow" button as shown in Fig. 8.1.

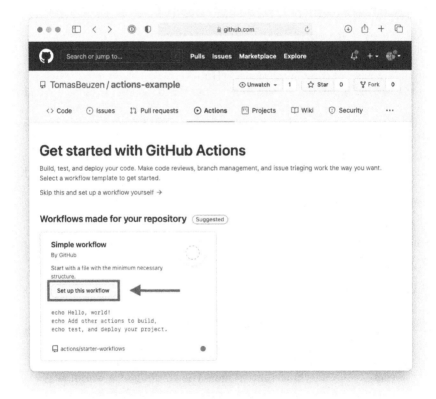

FIGURE 8.1: Setting up our first GitHub Actions workflow.

- **Step 2**

  Commit the *.yml* file that has been created for you to your repository by clicking "Start commit" and then "Commit new file". Then, open the file on GitHub. You should see the contents below. All the terminology we defined in **Section 8.3.1** exists in this workflow file, and each line is commented to describe exactly what it does. For example, we can see that:

- This workflow is triggered on any push or pull request made to the main branch.
- It consists of one job called build.
- The job will run on ubuntu-latest (the latest version of the Ubuntu runner GitHub Actions provides).
- It contains three steps. The first step "checks out" the repository — this is necessary for the runner to access your repository. The second step will print "Hello, world!" to the runner's terminal. The final step will print two lines. We'll discuss steps and how to write them in **Section 8.3.3**.

```
# This is a basic workflow to help you get started with Actions

# Name of the workflow
name: CI

# Controls when the workflow will run
on:
  # Triggers the workflow on push or pull request events but only for
  # the main branch
  push:
    branches: [ main ]
  pull_request:
    branches: [ main ]

  # Allows you to run this workflow manually from the Actions tab
  workflow_dispatch:

# A workflow run is made up of one or more jobs that can run
# sequentially or in parallel
jobs:
  # This workflow contains a single job called "build"
  build:
    # The type of runner that the job will run on
    runs-on: ubuntu-latest

    # Steps represent a sequence of tasks that will be executed as
    # part of the job
    steps:
      # Checks-out your repository so your job can access it
      - name: Check-out repository
        uses: actions/checkout@v2
```

```
# Runs a single command using the runners shell
- name: Run a one-line script
  run: echo Hello, world!

# Runs a set of commands using the runners shell
- name: Run a multi-line script
  run: |
      echo Add other actions to build,
      echo test, and deploy your project.
```

- **Step 3**

  Now, go to the "Actions" tab of your repository. You should see one workflow run, as in Fig. 8.2. This workflow ran because in **Step 2** we committed our workflow *.yml* file to the main branch of our repository, and the workflow is triggered to execute on any push or pull request with the main branch.

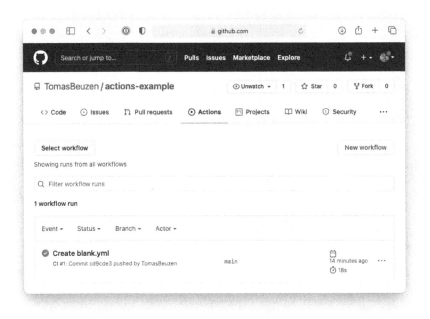

FIGURE 8.2: Our first GitHub Actions workflow.

- **Step 4**

  Look at the logs of the executed workflow by clicking on the "Create blank.yml" workflow, then clicking the "build" job in the left-hand panel.

Click on arrows inside the build logs to examine their output. You should be able to see output printed to the screen for the "Run a one-line script" and "Run a multi-line script" steps in our workflow, as shown in Fig. 8.3.

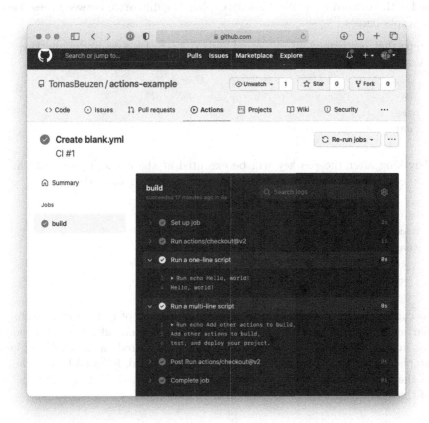

FIGURE 8.3: The logs of our first GitHub Actions workflow.

We'll practice writing workflows for implementing CI and CD for a Python package in the following sections of this chapter, but at this point, the high-level concepts to be aware of are:

- A workflow is a set of commands that are triggered to execute by certain events (like a push to the main branch of a repository).
- A workflow is run on a machine called a runner, which uses a particular operating system and is hosted by the CI/CD service.
- A workflow contains one or more jobs.
- Each job contains one or more steps to execute. In GitHub Actions, steps comprise either "actions" or "commands" as we'll discuss in the next section.

8.3.3   Actions and commands

As we saw in the workflow file in **Section 8.3.2**, a step in a GitHub Actions can be an "action" (specified with the keyword uses) or a "command" (specified with keyword run). We'll briefly explain the difference between these two concepts here.

Steps that use command line commands consist of a name and a run key, as shown in the example below:

```
# Runs a single command using the runners shell
- name: Run a one-line script
  run: echo Hello, world!
```

Anything after the run key will be executed at the runner's command line. You can run multiple commands in a single step using the | character:

```
# Runs a set of commands using the runners shell
- name: Run a multi-line script
  run: |
    echo Add other actions to build,
    echo test, and deploy your project.
```

In contrast to commands, actions are reusable units of code that perform a particular task without having to write out any commands. You'll typically use actions that have been created by others and shared on the GitHub Marketplace[7]. Actions are specified with the uses keyword, followed by the name of the action you want to use. The @ symbol is used to specify which version of the action you want to use, like in the example below:

```
# Checks-out your repository so your job can access it
- name: Check-out repository
  uses: actions/checkout@v2
```

Some actions can also be configured with inputs using the with key, as in the example below:

```
# Set up a Python environment for use in actions
- name: Set up Python
  uses: actions/setup-python@v2
  with:
    python-version: 3.9
```

---

[7]https://github.com/marketplace?type=

8.4 Setting up continuous integration

Now that we have a basic familiarity with GitHub Actions, in this section we'll build up a continuous integration workflow for a Python package. We'll create this workflow for the pycounts package we've been developing throughout this book. However, it will be applicable to any Python package, and it should be straightforward to see how you can modify it to your needs.

Our goal here is to create a CI workflow that will install our package with poetry, run our package's tests with pytest, and build its documentation with sphinx, every time someone makes a push or pull request of changes to the main branch of the pycounts GitHub repository. These are steps we, or a collaborator, would usually perform locally every time our package is changed, so it makes sense to automate them.

8.4.1 Setup

To set up a workflow with GitHub Actions, we need to create a workflow file. Workflow files are *.yml* files located in a *.github/workflows/* directory in the root package directory. We'll call our file *ci-cd.yml*. You can create that file in an editor of your choice, or by running the following commands at the command line, from your root package directory:

```
$ mkdir -p .github/workflows
$ touch .github/workflows/ci-cd.yml
```

Your package directory structure should now look something like the following:

```
pycounts
├── .github              <--------
│   └── workflows        <--------
│       └── ci-cd.yml    <--------
├── .readthedocs.yml
├── CHANGELOG.md
├── CONDUCT.md
├── CONTRIBUTING.md
├── docs
│   └── ...
├── LICENSE
├── README.md
├── poetry.lock
├── pyproject.toml
```

```
├── src
│   └── ...
└── tests
    └── ...
```

Open this new `ci-cd.yml` file in an editor. We are going to set up a CI workflow that triggers when someone pushes new content or makes a pull-request to any branch of our repository (note that this differs slightly to **Section 8.3.2**, where our workflow ran on push or pull request to the "main" branch only). To set this up, copy and paste the following text into `ci-cd.yml`:

When building our CI workflow, we'll be using the same syntax and terminology we described previously in **Section 8.3**. Don't be afraid to revise that section as needed.

```
name: ci-cd

on: [push, pull_request]
```

Now we need to set up the steps that will be executed if one of the above trigger events occurs. GitHub Actions essentially provides you with a blank operating system of your choice (a "runner"), which we need to set up based on what steps we are going to want it to execute. In our case, we need to install Python and install `poetry` on the runner, so that we can then install our packages and run its tests and build its documentation. Thus, our setup will involve the steps below, for which we've indicated whether step will use an action or command(s) (**Section 8.3.3**):

1. Specify an operating system. We'll be using Ubuntu with the syntax `runs-on: ubuntu-latest`. MacOS and Windows are also available if you wish to test your package on those systems, but Ubuntu is a good default to use — see the GitHub Actions documentation[8]).
2. Install Python (action: actions/setup-python@v2[9]).

---

[8]https://docs.github.com/en/actions/using-github-hosted-runners/about-github-hosted-runners#supported-runners-and-hardware-resources
[9]https://github.com/actions/setup-python

3. Checkout our repository so we can access its contents (action: actions/checkout@v2[10]).
4. Install poetry (action: snok/install-poetry@v1[11]).
5. Use poetry to install pycounts (command: poetry install).

We'll add all these steps to our workflow in a job called "ci":

```
name: ci-cd

on: [push, pull_request]

jobs:
  ci:
    # Set up operating system
    runs-on: ubuntu-latest

    # Define job steps
    steps:
    - name: Set up Python 3.9
      uses: actions/setup-python@v2
      with:
        python-version: 3.9

    - name: Check-out repository
      uses: actions/checkout@v2

    - name: Install poetry
      uses: snok/install-poetry@v1

    - name: Install package
      run: poetry install
```

The above steps will set up our system in preparation for:

1. Running pycounts's unit tests with pytest.
2. Checking the code coverage of our tests.
3. Checking that pycounts's documentation builds correctly.

We'll create each of these steps in the following sections.

---

[10]https://github.com/actions/checkout
[11]https://github.com/snok/install-poetry

8.4.2   Running tests

Remember all the hard work we put into writing tests for our package back in the **Chapter 5: Testing**? Well, we likely want to make sure that these tests (and any others that we add) continue to pass for any new changes proposed to our package.

Recall that we used `pytest` as the testing framework for our `pycounts` package. This is listed as a development dependency of our package, so it will already be installed on our runner from "Step 5" when we execute `poetry install`. Therefore, we just need to add a new step to our workflow with a command to run `pytest`. Because our runner is not using a `conda` virtual environment, `poetry` sets one up automatically when `poetry install` is executed. We need to explicitly tell `poetry` to use this virtual environment it set up for us by prefixing commands with `poetry run`, as we do below:

```
- name: Test with pytest
  run: poetry run pytest tests/ --cov=pycounts --cov-report=xml
```

We could install `conda` on our runner and set up a virtual environment if we wanted to. But this is a lot of overhead for a workflow that is just going to run tests and build documentation, so we've decided not to do that here.

Note that in the command above we are also obtaining our test coverage through the `--cov` argument and outputting a report to *.xml* format with the `--cov-report` argument (these require the `pytest-cov` package which we used and added as a dependency of our package in **Section 5.5.3**). In the next section, we will integrate another service called Codecov[12] into our workflow that will automatically record test coverage for us using the *.xml* report.

8.4.3   Recording code coverage

In the previous step, we ran the tests for our `pycounts` package. However, if someone adds new code to your package but forgets to write tests for that new code, your existing tests will still pass, but the coverage will be reduced. So, we probably want to track code coverage in our CI workflow.

---

[12]https://codecov.io/

To do this, we could print the coverage to our runner's build log, but having the coverage buried in those logs is not overly helpful. Instead, it's common to use a service like Codecov[13] to track our code coverage for us. To set up Codecov, first create a Codecov account by linking it with your GitHub account, as described in the Codecov documentation[14] (Codecov also supports GitLab and Bitbucket). Once you've done this, Codecov automatically syncs with all the repositories that you have access to. Now, to use Codecov to automatically track code coverage as part of our CI workflow we can use the action they've created called codecov/codecov-action@v2[15], as below:

If your GitHub repository is private, you'll need to provide an "upload token" to allow Codecov to access it as described in the Codecov documentation[16].

```
- name: Use Codecov to track coverage
  uses: codecov/codecov-action@v2
  with:
    files: ./coverage.xml    # coverage report
```

With this step in our workflow, coverage will automatically be recorded for each new proposed change to our code. Codecov can show you whether coverage has increased or decreased, by how much, and will link to relevant areas of your package's source code. This information will automatically appear on any pull request someone makes to the main branch on GitHub, or it can be viewed anytime on the Codecov website; for example, Fig. 8.4 shows the coverage dashboard for a package called pypkgs, where coverage decreased significantly after the most recent commit.

8.4.4 Build documentation

The final step we'll add to our CI workflow will be to check that our documentation builds without issue. We'll use the same make html command we've used throughout this book to build documentation with sphinx to do this:

---

[13]https://codecov.io/
[14]https://docs.codecov.com/docs
[15]https://github.com/marketplace/actions/codecov
[16]https://github.com/marketplace/actions/codecov

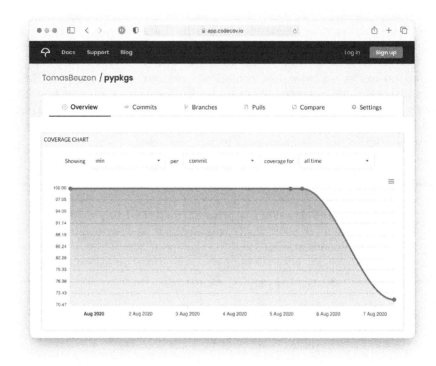

FIGURE 8.4: Example of the Codecov dashboard linked to a repository called pypkgs. Coverage decreased significantly after the most recent commit.

```
- name: Build documentation
  run: poetry run make html --directory docs/
```

8.4.5   Testing continuous integration

We've now set up our CI pipeline! Our final *.github/workflows/ci-cd.yml* file looks like this:

```
name: ci-cd

on: [push, pull_request]

jobs:
  ci:
    # Set up operating system
```

```
runs-on: ubuntu-latest

# Define job steps
steps:
- name: Set up Python 3.9
  uses: actions/setup-python@v2
  with:
    python-version: 3.9

- name: Check-out repository
  uses: actions/checkout@v2

- name: Install poetry
  uses: snok/install-poetry@v1

- name: Install package
  run: poetry install

- name: Test with pytest
  run: poetry run pytest tests/ --cov=pycounts --cov-report=xml

- name: Use Codecov to track coverage
  uses: codecov/codecov-action@v2
  with:
    files: ./coverage.xml   # coverage report

- name: Build documentation
  run: poetry run make html --directory docs/
```

We're now ready to test out our workflow! Let's go ahead and commit our workflow file to version control and push it to GitHub. This will trigger our workflow because we configured it to run when someone pushes new work to any branch of our repository.

```
$ git add .github/workflows/ci-cd.yml
$ git commit -m "build: add CI workflow"
$ git push
```

Now if we go to our `pycounts` GitHub repository and click on the "Actions" tab, we should see our workflow, as shown in Fig. 8.5:

We can investigate the build logs by clicking the "ci" job as in Fig. 8.6:

This workflow will trigger anytime someone makes a push or pull request with the `main` branch. Now you, or your collaborators, don't have to worry

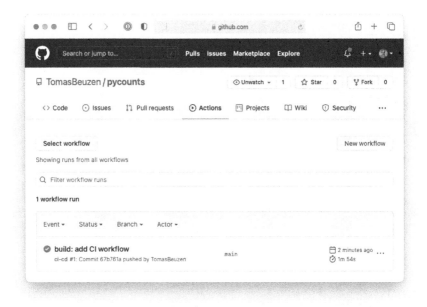

FIGURE 8.5: Successfully run continuous integration workflow on GitHub.

about remembering all these steps or running them manually! In the next section, we'll take this automation to the next level, and set up a workflow to automatically deploy a new version of our package if proposed changes pass the CI workflow.

8.5   Setting up continuous deployment

In the previous step, we set up CI for our package to check that tests run, code coverage is stable, and documentation still builds, whenever we make a push or pull request with new changes to the main branch of our repository.

In this section, we'll set up continuous deployment (CD). If the changes we push to our repository pass our CI, then we want a CD workflow that will automatically:

1. Create a new version of our pycounts package.
2. Build new distributions (i.e., sdist and wheel).
3. Upload the distributions to TestPyPI and test that the package can be installed successfully.

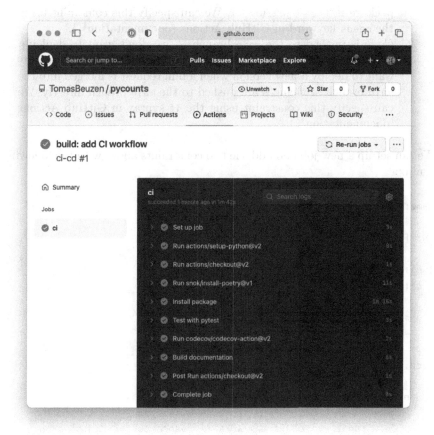

FIGURE 8.6: Continuous integration workflow logs.

4. Upload the distributions to PyPI.

We'll build up that CD workflow in this section.

8.5.1 Setup

To set up CD, we'll add to the *.github/workflows/ci-cd.yml* workflow file we created in **Section 8.4**. Our aim here is to add a new job called "cd" to this workflow that will trigger a deployment of our package each time updated code is pushed to the main branch of our repository. We only want this job to execute if:

1. The "ci" job passes — we don't want to deploy a new version of our

package if it isn't passing CI. We can specify this constraint using the needs keyword in GitHub Actions (documentation[17]).

2. Code is pushed to the main branch — we don't want to deploy a new version of our package when a pull request is opened, we only want to deploy a new version when a pull request is merged into the main branch or changes are pushed to the main branch directly. We can specify this constraint using the if syntax in GitHub Actions (documentation[18]).

We can set up a new job and add the two constraints above with the following syntax:

```
name: ci-cd

on: [push, pull_request]

jobs:
  ci:
    # ...
    # CI steps hidden
    # ...

  cd:
    # Only run this job if the "ci" job passes
    needs: ci

    # Only run this job if new work is pushed to the "main" branch
    if: github.event_name == 'push' && github.ref == 'refs/heads/main'
```

Now we can set up our CD workflow. In GitHub Actions, each job runs on a fresh runner, which we need to set up from scratch. Once we've done that, our CD workflow will effectively comprise all the steps we walked through manually in **Chapter 7: Releasing and versioning**. Below we list all the steps required to set up the CD workflow:

1. Specify an operating system. We'll be using Ubuntu again with the syntax runs-on: ubuntu-latest.
2. Install Python (action: actions/setup-python@v2[19]).

---

[17]https://docs.github.com/en/actions/reference/workflow-syntax-for-github-actions#jobsjob_idneeds
[18]https://docs.github.com/en/actions/reference/workflow-syntax-for-github-actions#jobsjob_idif
[19]https://github.com/actions/setup-python

3. Check out our repository so we can access its contents (action: actions/checkout@v2[20]).
4. Install poetry (action: snok/install-poetry@v1[21]).
5. Use poetry to install pycounts (command: poetry install).
6. Make a new release of pycounts (command: semantic-release publish, this uses the Python Semantic Release (PSR)[22] tool which we described in **Section 7.2.2** and will describe again below).
7. Upload new release to TestPyPI (action: pypa/gh-action-pypi-publish@release/v1[23]).
8. Test that the new package version installs successfully from TestPyPI (command: pip install).
9. Upload new release to PyPI (action: pypa/gh-action-pypi-publish@release/v1[24]).

Steps 1 to 5 are the same as we set up previously for our CI workflow, so we can just copy and paste them into our "cd" job as below. The only new code here is that we specify the input parameter fetch-depth: 0 for the actions/checkout@v2[25] action. This input parameter will allow the PSR tool to access the full history of commits in our repository, so that it can determine how to bump the package's version. Without this parameter, PSR can only access the single most recent commit message.

```
name: ci-cd

on: [push, pull_request]

jobs:
  ci:
    # ...
    # CI steps hidden
    # ...

  cd:
    # Only run this job if the "ci" job passes
    needs: ci

    # Only run this job if new work is pushed to "main"
    if: github.event_name == 'push' && github.ref == 'refs/heads/main'
```

---
[20]https://github.com/actions/checkout
[21]https://github.com/snok/install-poetry
[22]https://python-semantic-release.readthedocs.io/en/latest/
[23]https://github.com/pypa/gh-action-pypi-publish
[24]https://github.com/pypa/gh-action-pypi-publish
[25]https://github.com/actions/checkout

```
# Set up operating system
runs-on: ubuntu-latest

# Define job steps
steps:
  - name: Set up Python 3.9
    uses: actions/setup-python@v2
    with:
      python-version: 3.9

  - name: Check-out repository
    uses: actions/checkout@v2
    with:
      fetch-depth: 0

  - name: Install poetry
    uses: snok/install-poetry@v1

  - name: Install package
    run: poetry install
```

We'll discuss steps 6 to 9 in the sections below.

8.5.2 Automatically creating a new package version

As we saw in **Chapter 7: Releasing and versioning**, there are a few key steps to go through when creating a new version of your package:

1. Document what's changed in the CHANGELOG.md.
2. Bump the package version number.
3. Tag a new release on GitHub.
4. Build a new sdist and wheel.

In **Section 7.2.2**, we introduced the Python Semantic Release (PSR)[26] tool, which can automatically bump your package's version number based on keywords it finds in commit messages.

However, PSR can do more than this! In fact, it can do all the steps we list above. In **Section 7.2.2**, we saw how PSR is configured using a table called [tool.semantic_release] in the *pyproject.toml*. To configure it to perform all the steps above, we need to add a few keys to that table as follows:

---

[26]https://python-semantic-release.readthedocs.io/en/latest/

```
[tool.semantic_release]
version_variable = "pyproject.toml:version"  # version location
branch = "main"                              # branch to make releases of
changelog_file = "CHANGELOG.md"              # changelog file
build_command = "poetry build"               # build dists
dist_path = "dist/"                          # where to put dists
upload_to_release = true                     # auto-create GitHub release
upload_to_pypi = false                       # don't auto-upload to PyPI
remove_dist = false                          # don't remove dists
patch_without_tag = true                     # patch release by default
```

We've added comments above to clarify what each key is doing in the table, and we describe them in Table 8.2. You can also read more about these configuration options in the PSR documentation[27].

TABLE 8.2: Description of Python Semantic Release configuration options.

Key	Description
version_variable	Location of version number for PSR to bump.
branch	Branch where releases should be made from.
changelog_file	Location of changelog file for PSR to update using commit messages.
build_command	How to build new distributions for the release.
dist_path	Location of distributions after running build_command.
upload_to_release	Whether to automatically create a release of the new package version on GitHub.
upload_to_pypi	Whether to upload to PyPI. Default is true, but we want to upload to TestPyPI first to test things out, so we've turned this off.
remove_dist	Whether to remove distributions at dist_path after upload. We turned this off because we want to upload these distributions to TestPyPI and PyPI ourselves.

---

[27]https://python-semantic-release.readthedocs.io/en/latest/configuration.html

Key	Description
patch_without_tag	Always create a new patch release even if there is no trigger tag, such as "fix" or "feat", in any commits since the last release.

With PSR configured in our *pyproject.toml*, we can now add it as a step to our CD workflow.

In **Section 7.2.2**, we used the command `semantic-release version` to get PSR to automatically update our version based on keywords it finds in all the commit messages that have been made since the last tag of your package. In our CD workflow, we'll be using the slightly different command `semantic-release publish`, which will bump our version, update our changelog, tag a new release on GitHub, and build a new sdist and wheel.

PSR will need to interact with our GitHub repository to modify our *CHANGELOG.md* file and tag a new release of our package. To give PSR permission to do this there's a few things we need to do:

1. Provide PSR with a GitHub access token[28] called `GH_TOKEN` to allow it to read/write files in our repository. At the start of each workflow run, GitHub automatically creates[29] such a token for us, called `GITHUB_TOKEN`. We can pass this token to PSR using the env key and the syntax `${{ secrets.GITHUB_TOKEN }}`. You can read more about this syntax in the GitHub documentation[30], but we've done it for you in the code shown below.

2. Configure the Git credentials of the runner machine by setting the username as `github-actions` and email address as `github-actions@github.com`. If you don't configure these credentials, the workflow won't be able to make changes to our repository, as you can read more about in the GitHub documentation[31]. We've also done this for you in the code shown below, so all you need to do is add this code as the next step in your CD workflow file.

```
- name: Use Python Semantic Release to prepare release
  env:
```

---

[28]https://python-semantic-release.readthedocs.io/en/latest/envvars.html#env-gh-token

[29]https://docs.github.com/en/actions/security-guides/automatic-token-authentication

[30]https://docs.github.com/en/actions/security-guides/encrypted-secrets#using-encrypted-secrets-in-a-workflow

[31]https://docs.github.com/en/get-started/getting-started-with-git/setting-your-username-in-git

```
      GH_TOKEN: ${{ secrets.GITHUB_TOKEN }}
    run: |
        git config user.name github-actions
        git config user.email github-actions@github.com
        poetry run semantic-release publish
```

We'll see PSR in action shortly, but let's first configure the rest of our CD workflow file.

8.5.3   Uploading to TestPyPI and PyPI

The PSR step will create an sdist and wheel for our new package version. What we need to do next in our CD workflow is try uploading those distributions to TestPyPI. This step is not strictly necessary, but it's a good idea because it can help catch any unexpected errors before we upload our package to PyPI.

Rather than write the code needed to do all this from scratch, we'll use the pypa/gh-action-pypi-publish@release/v1[32] action. This action relies on token authentication with TestPyPI (rather than the classic username and password authentication). To use the action, you'll need to log-in to TestPyPI[33], create an API token[34], and add the token as a secret[35] called TEST_PYPI_API_TOKEN to your GitHub repository, as shown in Fig. 8.7.

To use the pypa/gh-action-pypi-publish@release/v1[36] action, we can add the following step to our CD workflow. Note how we configure the action to use the token user method, specifying password as the TEST_PYPI_API_TOKEN we just added to our repository, and we point the action to the TestPyPI repository (repository_url: https://test.pypi.org/legacy/).

```
  - name: Publish to TestPyPI
    uses: pypa/gh-action-pypi-publish@release/v1
    with:
        user: __token__
        password: ${{ secrets.TEST_PYPI_API_TOKEN }}
        repository_url: https://test.pypi.org/legacy/
```

The above action will publish the new version of your package to TestPyPI. We now want to test that we can install the package correctly from TestPyPI using the following command:

---

[32] https://github.com/pypa/gh-action-pypi-publish
[33] https://test.pypi.org
[34] https://pypi.org/help/#apitoken
[35] https://docs.github.com/en/actions/reference/encrypted-secrets
[36] https://github.com/pypa/gh-action-pypi-publish

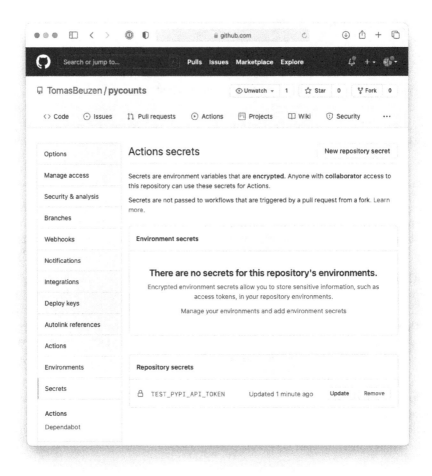

FIGURE 8.7: Adding the TestPyPI API token to our GitHub repository.

```
- name: Test install from TestPyPI
  run: |
      pip install \
      --index-url https://test.pypi.org/simple/ \
      --extra-index-url https://pypi.org/simple \
      pycounts
```

Finally, the last step in our CD workflow will be publishing our package to PyPI. This uses the same pypa/gh-action-pypi-publish@release/v1[37] action as

---

[37]https://github.com/pypa/gh-action-pypi-publish

earlier and will require you to obtain a token from PyPI[38] and add the token as `PYPI_API_TOKEN` to your GitHub repository, as shown in Fig. 8.8.

```
- name: Publish to PyPI
  uses: pypa/gh-action-pypi-publish@release/v1
  with:
    user: __token__
    password: ${{ secrets.PYPI_API_TOKEN }}
```

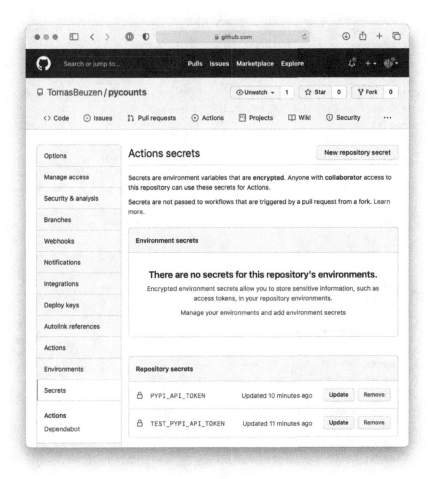

FIGURE 8.8: Adding the PyPI API token to our GitHub repository.

---

[38]https://pypi.org

8.5.4   Testing continuous deployment

We've now set up our CD workflow! Our final *.github/workflows/ci-cd.yml* file looks like this:

```yaml
name: ci-cd

on: [push, pull_request]

jobs:
  ci:
    # ...
    # CI steps same as before
    # ...

  cd:
    # Only run this job if the "ci" job passes
    needs: ci

    # Only run this job if new work is pushed to "main"
    if: github.event_name == 'push' && github.ref == 'refs/heads/main'

    # Set up operating system
    runs-on: ubuntu-latest

    # Define job steps
    steps:
    - name: Set up Python 3.9
      uses: actions/setup-python@v2
      with:
        python-version: 3.9

    - name: Check-out repository
      uses: actions/checkout@v2
      with:
        fetch-depth: 0

    - name: Install poetry
      uses: snok/install-poetry@v1

    - name: Install package
      run: poetry install

    - name: Use Python Semantic Release to prepare release
      env:
```

```
    GH_TOKEN: ${{ secrets.GITHUB_TOKEN }}
run: |
    git config user.name github-actions
    git config user.email github-actions@github.com
    poetry run semantic-release publish

- name: Publish to TestPyPI
  uses: pypa/gh-action-pypi-publish@release/v1
  with:
    user: __token__
    password: ${{ secrets.TEST_PYPI_API_TOKEN }}
    repository_url: https://test.pypi.org/legacy/

- name: Test install from TestPyPI
  run: |
    pip install \
    --index-url https://test.pypi.org/simple/ \
    --extra-index-url https://pypi.org/simple \
    pycounts

- name: Publish to PyPI
  uses: pypa/gh-action-pypi-publish@release/v1
  with:
    user: __token__
    password: ${{ secrets.PYPI_API_TOKEN }}
```

We're now ready to test out our full CI/CD workflow! Let's go ahead and commit our new workflow file and our *pyproject.toml* file (which we changed when we added the configuration options for PSR) to version control and push it to GitHub. This will trigger our CI/CD workflow because we configured it to run when someone pushes to the "main" branch of our repository. For the sake of example, we'll include the "feat" keyword in our commit message to trigger PSR to make a minor release of our package from these changes.

We described what keywords trigger particular version bumps in **Section 7.2.2**, but note that even if no keywords were present in any commits, we configured PSR in **Section 8.5.2** to make a patch release by default.

```
$ git add .github/workflows/ci-cd.yml pyproject.toml
$ git commit -m "feat: add CI/CD workflow"
$ git push
```

Now if we go to our `pycounts` GitHub repository and click on the "Actions" tab, we should see a new run of our workflow as shown in Fig. 8.9:

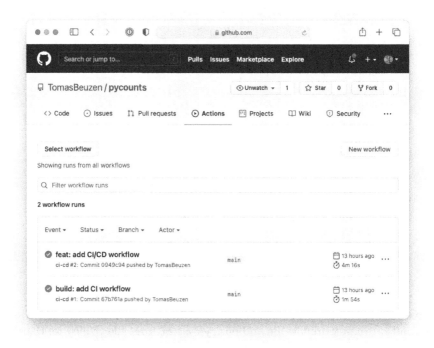

FIGURE 8.9: Continuous deployment workflow on GitHub.

If we click on the workflow we will see it was composed of two jobs, "ci" and "cd", each of which ran successfully, as shown in Fig. 8.10:

If we click on the "cd" job to view the build log, we can see that PSR parsed our commit message — "feat: add CI/CD workflow" — to determine that our package should be bumped with a minor release from 0.2.0 to 0.3.0 as shown in Fig. 8.11.

PSR also automatically updated our changelog and tagged a new release of our package, as shown in Fig. 8.12 and Fig. 8.13, respectively.

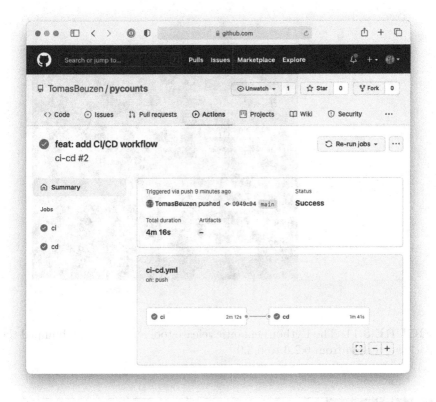

FIGURE 8.10: Successfully run continuous deployment workflow on GitHub.

Finally, we can see from the build logs that the new version of our package was released to TestPyPI and PyPI, as shown in Fig. 8.14:

It didn't take too long for us to implement a CD workflow that completely automates all the steps we would usually have to perform manually when publishing a new release of our package. You may choose, or need, to use different tools and commands to what we've used here to implement CD for your packages in the future. But hopefully you can see the kinds of things that are possible with CD and how it can be useful to quickly deploy new releases of your package, how it saves you from having to remember all the commands you'd need to run to do this yourself, and how it lowers the barrier for potential collaborators to contribute to your package.

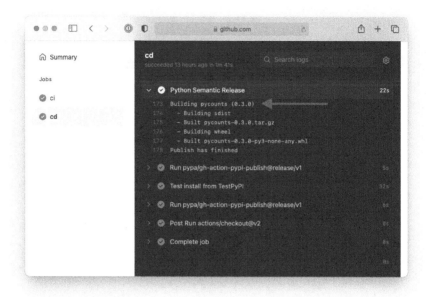

FIGURE 8.11: The Python semantic release tool automatically bumped the package version from 0.2.0 to 0.3.0.

8.6   Summary

In this chapter, we created CI/CD workflows for our pycounts package. What we've shown here is just one example and one set of tools for implementing CI/CD — but after reading this chapter, the hope is that you can appreciate the utility of CI/CD and the kinds of workflows that you can set up for your packages in the future.

It's important to note that when using version control in this book, we've been directly modifying the main branch of our repository. However, changes to your package are more typically made on branches. Branches isolate your changes so you can develop your package without affecting the existing, stable version. Only when you're happy with your changes and they've passed CI, do you merge them into the existing source and trigger a CD workflow (if it exists). In collaborative environments, this is typically done via a "pull request", which you can read more about in the GitHub documentation[39]. Open-source projects are built off pull requests; go visit your favorite Python

---

[39]https://docs.github.com/en/github/collaborating-with-pull-requests/proposing-changes-to-your-work-with-pull-requests/about-pull-requests

FIGURE 8.12: The Python semantic release tool automatically updated the changelog and added an entry for v0.3.0 based on commit messages.

package repository on GitHub and click the "Pull requests" tab to see what and how collaborators are merging changes into the package, and the kind of CI/CD workflows that are set up to handle them.

Finally, while we developed our workflow file from scratch here, the py-pkgs-cookiecutter template[40] we used to set up our package in **Section 3.2.2** can make the workflow *.yml* file for you. Recall from **Section 3.2.2** that one of the py-pkgs-cookiecutter prompts was as follows:

```
Select include_github_actions:
1 - no
```

---

[40]https://github.com/py-pkgs/py-pkgs-cookiecutter

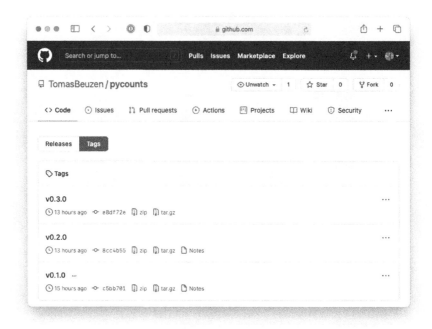

FIGURE 8.13: The Python semantic release tool automatically created tagged release v0.3.0.

```
2 - ci
3 - ci+cd
Choose from 1, 2, 3 [1]:
```

In the future, you can include a workflow file for CI or CI+CD by selecting an appropriate response.

Congratulations on making it to the end of the book and happy packaging!

FIGURE 8.14: Deployment of new package version 0.3.0 to PyPI.

Bibliography

Abbott, E. A. (1884). *Flatland*. Seeley and Co.

Bryan, J., Hester, J., and Assistants, S. T. (2021). Happy git and GitHub for the user. https://happygitwithr.com/.

Fucci, D., Erdogmus, H., Turhan, B., Oivo, M., and Juristo, N. (2016). A dissection of the test-driven development process: Does it really matter to test-first or to test-last? *IEEE Transactions on Software Engineering*, 43(7):597–614.

Harris, C. R., Millman, K. J., van der Walt, S. J., Gommers, R., Virtanen, P., Cournapeau, D., Wieser, E., Taylor, J., Berg, S., Smith, N. J., Kern, R., Picus, M., Hoyer, S., van Kerkwijk, M. H., Brett, M., Haldane, A., del Río, J. F., Wiebe, M., Peterson, P., Gérard-Marchant, P., Sheppard, K., Reddy, T., Weckesser, W., Abbasi, H., Gohlke, C., and Oliphant, T. E. (2020). Array programming with NumPy. *Nature*, 585(7825):357–362.

Hunter, J. D. (2007). Matplotlib: A 2d graphics environment. *Computing in Science & Engineering*, 9(3):90–95.

Irving, D., Hertweck, K., Johnston, L., Ostblom, J., Wickham, C., and Wilson, G. (2021). *Research Software Engineering with Python*. Chapman and Hall/CRC.

Kluyver, T., Ragan-Kelley, B., Pérez, F., Granger, B. E., Bussonnier, M., Frederic, J., Kelley, K., Hamrick, J. B., Grout, J., Corlay, S., et al. (2016). *Jupyter Notebooks-a publishing format for reproducible computational workflows.*, volume 2016. IOS Press.

The Carpentries (2021). Plotting and programming in Python: Writing functions. https://swcarpentry.github.io/python-novice-gapminder/16-writing-functions/index.html.

Wickham, H. and Bryan, J. (2015). *R Packages*. O'Reilly Media, Inc.

Index

Printed in the United States
by Baker & Taylor Publisher Services

Printed in the United States
by Baker & Taylor Publisher Services